W9-AXB-431

FINISHING TOUCHES

TOUCHES

WITH

Paint & Paper

FINISHING TOUCHES
WITH
*Paint &
Paper*

EMMA, JOSEPHINE
AND CATHERINE WHITFIELD

PENGUIN
STUDIO

CHESTERFIELD COUNTY LIBRARY

For Jack, Grace and Patrick

PENGUIN STUDIO
Published by the Penguin Group
Penguin Books USA Inc., 375 Hudson Street,
New York, New York, 10014, U.S.A.

Penguin Books Ltd, 27 Wrights Lane,
London W8 5TZ, England

Penguin Books Australia Ltd, Ringwood,
Victoria, Australia

Penguin Books Canada Ltd, 2801 John Street,
Markham, Ontario, Canada L3R 1B4

Penguin Books (N.Z.) Ltd, 182-90 Wairau Road,
Auckland 10, New Zealand

Penguin Books Ltd, Registered Offices:
Harmondsworth, Middlesex, England

First published by Penguin Studio, an imprint of Penguin Books USA Inc.
First printing, January 1997
10 9 8 7 6 5 4 3 2 1

Copyright text, illustrations and compilation © 1996 Carroll & Brown
Copyright project designs © 1996 Emma, Josephine and Catherine Whitfield
All rights reserved.

Without limiting the rights under copyright reserved above, no part of this publication
may be reproduced, stored in or introduced into a retrieval system, or transmitted, in
any form, or by any means (electronic, mechanical, photocopying, recording, or
otherwise), without the prior written permission of both the copyright owner and the
publisher of the book.

Library of Congress Catalog Card Number: 96-68907
ISBN: 0-670-87296-2

Created by
CARROLL & BROWN LIMITED
5 Lonsdale Road
London NW6 6RA

PUBLISHING DIRECTOR DENIS KENNEDY
ART DIRECTOR CHRISSIE LLOYD
PROJECT EDITOR SANDY CARR
ART EDITOR MERCEDES MORGAN
DESIGNER SUSAN KNIGHT
PHOTOGRAPHY DAVID MURRAY
PRODUCTION WENDY ROGERS, KATE DISNEY

Reproduced by Colourscan, Singapore
Printed and bound by L.E.G.O. Vicenza, Italy

*The designs in this book may not be produced commercially without the prior permission
in writing of the copyright owner. When photocopying images for use in craft works, please take note
of the laws affecting copyright. Every effort has been made to ensure that the instructions given in this
book are completely safe and accurate, but the copyright owners cannot accept liability for any resulting
injury, damage or loss to persons or property that may occur.*

CONTENTS

◆

Introduction

Papier mâché *Bright bowls, page 126.*

*M*aking things is one of the great pleasures of life. Experimenting with designs, colors and materials is endlessly absorbing. Apart from beautifying your own surroundings, it is also very satisfying to be able to make original personal gifts for your family and friends.

This book features five of the most versatile crafts: découpage, decorative paint effects, stenciling, paper cut-outs and papier mâché. With all these crafts it is possible to achieve impressive results quickly with very little previous experience. Step-by-step instructions explain the techniques clearly. Some projects are very simple – a découpaged mini-chest or a stenciled chair, for example. Others are more ambitious and will require a little more time and patience.

Paint effects *Gilded frames, page 62.*

In all cases full use is made of modern materials, especially water-based paints and varnishes, which are easier and safer to use than traditional oil-based products as well as being quick-drying – an important consideration if you are trying to fit your craft work into the diminishing spaces in a busy life. A few projects require specialist equipment and materials, but most can be accomplished with the kinds of things you will find in every home. Almost any surface can be decorated with paint and paper – from

Découpage *Hat boxes, page 28.*

a small gift box to the walls of an entire room. We have concentrated on small items of furniture and accessories – wall cupboards, shelves, mini-chests, little boxes, containers of various kinds, picture frames, flower pots. The illustrated List of Projects on the following pages is grouped by type of object and it will help you decide what to make, but many of the ideas here are easily adaptable to larger things. There is a comprehensive template section at the back of the book, and motifs and stencils can be multiplied or scaled up. Techniques such as gilding, crackle finishes and distressing paintwork can be applied to doors and chests of drawers as well as to frames, letter racks and utensil holders.

Paper cut-outs *Shining shades, page 114.*

You can vary the color schemes too, to fit in with your own tastes and your own home. Don't be afraid to experiment with color because you can always repaint something if it goes wrong. Inspiration for color combinations can come from all sorts of places. Ideas for colors and designs can be drawn from a mixture of sources – from nature, from visits to museums, from the world around you. A leaf or a piece of Byzantine pottery or a Renaissance painting might suggest a motif or color scheme.

There are over 70 projects in the book and whether you are a novice or a seasoned craftsperson, we hope you will find something here to interest or intrigue you. We hope, too, that you will be inspired by the projects to take off on your own creative adventure, devising your own designs and using the skills you have acquired here in a host of new and original ways.

Stenciling *Canal cans, page 80.*

Round boxes

Plain round and oval boxes come in many sizes, from small ones, perfect for storing little pieces of jewelry or beads, to large hat boxes.

Rectangular boxes

A collection of small and medium-sized storage boxes is decorated in a wide variety of styles and techniques – découpage, stencils, paper cut-outs.

Bins and containers

Every home needs a miscellany of containers for temporary or long-term storage or for display. These range from pencil-holders to wastepaper bins.

Containers
page 32
Cylindrical holders for pencils or paint brushes are découpaged with geometric borders.

Boat bin
page 46
A breezy storage bin for a child's room has a painted seascape with découpaged shells and sailing ships.

Hearts bin
page 118
Hearts cut out of colored paper decorate a four-sided container that can double as an umbrella stand.

Filigree bin
page 119
Cleverly cut from folded paper, delicate colored motifs with an Oriental feel cover a practical storage or wastepaper bin.

Frames

Frames are an ideal vehicle for interesting paint effects – especially gilding. There are also some intriguing découpage and papier-mâché designs.

Grapes and vines
page 34
Trailing vines and bunches of grapes grace this mellow pictorial frame.

Pastoral scene
page 34
A découpaged landscape of forests and meadows with cows peacefully grazing covers a wide wooden frame.

Silver frame
page 62
Stripes of rust and silver leaf decorate a plain frame.

Molded frame
page 62
A classic molded wooden frame is burnished with bronze metallic powder.

Spattered frame
page 63
Spattering on a gilded frame produces an interesting patinated finish.

Gold scroll frame
page 132
Papier mâché layered on top of a thick card mold is built up into a three-dimensional shaped frame.

Green deco frame
page 133
A simple rectangular frame with a design of papier-mâché relief shapes painted in greens and copper.

Mini-chests

Small chests of drawers can be decorated to fit into any part of the house. These are designed for kitchens, bedrooms, studies, or children's rooms.

Shelves and wall fittings

Découpage and paint effects can liven up even the most utilitarian accessories such as racks to hang your hat on and kitchen-utensil holders.

Lampshades

Plain shades provide a canvas for stenciled fish and shells, and paper cut-out collages.

Tables and chairs

Small pieces of furniture such as chairs and tables can be given a bright new lease on life with découpage and stenciled decoration.

Circus chair
page 47
Jolly découpaged clowns peep out behind a Big Top curtain.

Tulip chair
page 94
Stencil bright pink tulips on a plain wooden chair.

Chess table
page 102
Stencils and cut-out board make an elegant games table.

Cupboards

A clutch of versatile cupboards is given a variety of attractive decorative treatments.

Wild strawberries
page 42
Luscious red strawberries are découpaged around a heart.

Drums cupboard
page 43
Découpaged drums combine with hand-painted drumsticks.

Check cupboard
page 70
Vibrant paint effects decorate a square cupboard.

Bathroom cabinet
page 98
An anchor motif is stenciled on a colorwashed cupboard.

Bowls, plates and vases

A collection of colorful papier-mâché crockery is decorated with hand-painted geometric patterns, stencils, paper cut-outs and découpage.

Urn
page 124
Hand-paint wavy stripes on a Greek-style vase.

Hexagonal vase
page 125
Paper cut-out diamond shapes pepper a decorative vase.

Spirals bowl
page 128
A golden yellow bowl is stenciled with swirling spirals in green, red and purple.

Zigzag bowl
page 128
A round blue bowl is given a trimmed zigzag edge and painted with sizzling stripes.

Patchwork bowl
page 129
Multi-colored paper shapes cover a small round chalice-like bowl cleverly raised on a conical base.

Square plate
page 130
Paper cut-outs decorate a plate in strong pastel colors.

Oval plate
page 131
Sprinkle a pretty blue plate with découpage flower heads.

Trays

Plain wooden trays are ideal vehicles for decoration. These show a range of techniques and styles from traditional vinegar-painting to paper cut-outs.

Buckets and cans

Metal watering cans, buckets and plant containers can also be decorated. Stenciling and paint effects are the most appropriate techniques.

Flower pots

Unglazed clay pots destined for indoor use can be painted successfully. Try these pretty stenciled flower pots for starters.

Trailing ivy trough
page 92
A combination of stenciling and spattering produces a delicate variegated ivy motif which works perfectly on an oval flower trough.

Swag pot
page 93
Two colorways are suggested for a simple, strong stenciled swag design repeated all around the pots.

Toyboxes

These large storage chests require something special. They are useful not only for toys, but for other large items that need tucking away.

Carousel toybox
page 44
Inspired by exuberant fairground decoration, this chest is covered in découpaged scrolls, borders and carousel horses.

Sports chest
page 96
A stenciled tennis match decorates a storage box for sporting gear.

Letter racks and stationery

Stationery items such as notepaper and envelopes, gift boxes, bags and tags are given an individual touch with simple stenciling and paint effects.

Beetle letter rack
page 54
A letter rack is finished with a crackle glaze that produces an attractive effect of peeling paint.

Gift bag
page 56
Gently sponged autumnal textures and leaf stencils are worked on gift bags in two colorways. Leaf gift tags are made to match.

Gift box
page 57
Reverse stencils and stippling with gold metallic powder decorate a card gift box.

Scroll letter rack
page 76
Extravagant scrolls are stenciled in various combinations all over a plain letter rack.

Stationery
page 76
Scroll stencils are used for instant decoration on notepaper and envelopes.

Basic know-how

Wonderful effects can be created with the kinds of materials that are in every home — little in the way of specialist equipment is needed — and the basic skills of preparation and finishing are the same as for ordinary household use.

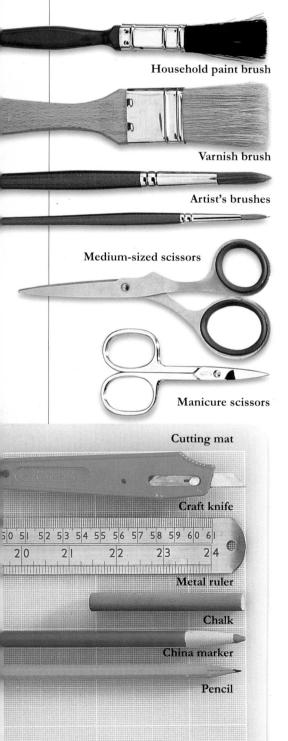

Household paint brush

Varnish brush

Artist's brushes

Medium-sized scissors

Manicure scissors

Cutting mat

Craft knife

Metal ruler

Chalk

China marker

Pencil

EQUIPMENT

There is a lot of mystique about craft equipment. Sometimes a specialist tool makes all the difference to a task but mostly you can find everything you need in a domestic tool box or an ordinary do-it-yourself shop. Where specialist tools are needed, they are listed in the relevant chapter.

Paint and varnish brushes

Paint is usually, though not always, applied with brushes.

Household paint brushes For most of the uses in this book ordinary household paint brushes are perfectly adequate. Needed most often will be the smaller sizes, up to 3in (75mm). They are used for applying not only paint, but also for varnishes and adhesives. Keep brushes for each material separately, and one set just for white paint. Brushes come in various qualities of natural bristle and synthetic fibers. Buy the best you can afford. Cheap brushes shed hairs freely and lose their shape quickly. You will need to replace them more often than good brushes which will last a long time if cared for.

Varnish brushes For crafts like découpage, which involve many careful applications of varnish, it is worth investing in special varnishing brushes. These are flatter than ordinary brushes, and make it easier to apply the varnish smoothly and evenly without brushmarks. They must be kept immaculately clean and never be used for anything else.

Artist's brushes A set of these in various sizes has many uses. Very little free-hand painting is involved in the projects, but you may sometimes need to add fine detail to a stenciled motif, or to hand-tint a monochrome motif for découpage, or to paint in ruled borders or edgings. Again there are various qualities. The cheaper camel or squirrel-hair brushes are good enough for most tasks.

Cutting tools

Many of the projects involve cutting out templates, motifs or stencils.

Scissors Straight-bladed household scissors will cope with many cutting jobs. Keep a pair specially for paper-cutting and have them sharpened regularly. Small straight and curved manicure scissors are also helpful for cutting intricate shapes.

Craft knife Craft knives or scalpels with replacement blades are invaluable. Use them for cutting intricate, delicate and complex shapes where scissors would be cumbersome, also for cutting heavier materials such as clear acetate for stencils, thick card or corrugated card. Replace the blades frequently. Keep your fingers away from the cutting edge and keep knife and blades out of reach of small children.

Cutting mat For crafts which involve a lot of cutting, it is worth investing in a self-healing cutting mat.

Metal ruler Use this with a craft knife and cutting mat for cutting dead straight edges.

Drawing and marking tools

A variety of pencils and markers are needed for drawing up and tracing designs and marking position guides.

Pencils Use ordinary soft pencils or china markers for drawing up position guides for designs or tracing round templates onto the object. Use harder pencils for tracing designs or templates, and for transferring resized motifs on to the relevant paper.

Pens A permanent black marker pen with a fine point is needed for tracing stencils on to clear acetate.

Chalk Use this for marking guidelines, registration marks or tracing round template shapes onto surfaces.

Masking tape Artist's tape is invaluable for masking straight edges of panels or borders to be painted in contrasting colors. Use it also to hold stencils, templates or motifs in place temporarily.

Other equipment

Sponges Paint can also be applied with a sponge – not only for a special decorative sponged effect, but also simply for a slightly textured rather than a smooth brushed finish. Natural sponges are best for this purpose. Flat household synthetic sponges can be cut into printing blocks. They are also useful for wiping down surfaces prior to painting and for cleaning off surplus adhesive.

Cloths Clean cotton lint-free cloths are used for ragging on and off, for applying color washes, colored varnish or wax and for cleaning up generally after a project.

Sandpaper You will need plenty of this in several grades: coarser papers for rubbing back bare wood, and progressively finer grades for smoothing painted surfaces and for sanding down varnish between coats. Sandpaper can also be used to rough up smooth surfaces to provide grip for repainting.

Steel wool also comes in various grades. It is especially useful for rubbing down metal surfaces. Wipe down the surface well after using it to remove any tiny filaments left behind.

Saucers and small bowls are useful for mixing small quantities of paint.

MATERIALS

Paint, paper, adhesives and varnish are the basic requirements for most of the projects. Where more rarefied materials are needed, they are described in the introduction to each chapter.

Paint

Wherever possible water-based paints have been used. They have the considerable advantage of being non-toxic and quick-drying. Since water is the solvent, it can also be used for thinning the paint and for cleaning brushes afterwards. However, it also means that all decorative work must be thoroughly sealed with varnish to protect and preserve it.

Latex paint This is a water-based paint available in either mat or silk-vinyl finishes. It is ideal for base coats and can also be used for paint effects and for stenciling or printing. It is available in a huge variety of colors from the palest pastels to rich dark shades. They can often be obtained in small sample pots which are perfect for small-scale decorative work. You can also mix latex paints yourself or add colorizers or small quantities of acrylic paint to obtain a particular color. The paint is normally used undiluted from the can, but it can also be diluted with water for color washes or mixed with scumble glaze to delay drying.

Acrylic paint Artists' acrylic paints are fast-drying, intense, water-based colors, which when dry have a more plastic quality than latex. They are more expensive, but are available in tubes, and are used in small quantities for things like stenciling, hand-painting, paint effects and so on. They can be mixed with scumble glaze or water for color washes and to delay drying for broken colorwork. Metallic shades such as gold, bronze, copper and silver are very effective. Artist's gouache can be used instead of acrylic, but it is even more expensive.

Powder paint Powdered dry pigment is occasionally needed especially for vinegar-painting. It is inexpensive and

Sandpaper   Cloth   Steel wool

Acrylic paint   Latex paint   Natural sponge

White Craft Glue

Colored varnish

Clear varnish

Decorative papers

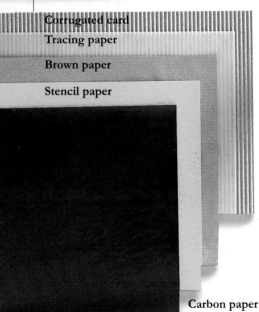

Corrugated card

Tracing paper

Brown paper

Stencil paper

Carbon paper

can be mixed with water or with acrylic gel medium.

Oil-based paints Use enamel paint on metal surfaces. It does not need varnishing afterwards, though you will need to varnish any decorative work – stenciling, for example – carried out with acrylic on top. Artist's oil paints have a variety of uses in decorative paint techniques.

Primers Bare surfaces usually need to be primed before painting. Use the appropriate primers for wood and metal (see page 17).

Varnishes

Varnishes are essential to seal and protect decorative paint and paper work, especially where water-based paints are used.

Acrylic varnish Clear acrylic varnish can be used in most cases. It is water-based, quick-drying and does not yellow with time, but is not as hard-wearing as polyurethane varnishes so more coats will be needed. It is available in gloss, satin, mat and dead-flat finishes. Colored acrylic varnishes are also obtainable. Acrylic varnishes can be used only over other water-based products.

Polyurethane varnish This will be necessary where the base coat or decoration has been executed in an oil-based product. It is very hard-wearing but takes longer to dry than acrylic varnish and tends to yellow a little with time. It is available in gloss, satin and mat finishes, and clear or colored. Polyurethane varnishes can also be used over water-based paints if required, and for a durable finish apply a couple of extra coats of polyurethane on top of a sequence of acrylic varnishings.

Adhesives

Adhesives are needed for découpage, paper cut-outs and papier mâché.

White Craft Glue is also sometimes sold as wood glue. It is ideal for most paper-sticking jobs.
It can also be diluted and used as a print sealer and as a light varnish. Apply it with a spatula or brush.

Wallpaper paste is an inexpensive alternative adhesive to white craft glue.

Paper

Paper is among the most versatile of materials. Here it is used broadly in two ways: for practical purposes and decoratively. In the first category are such specialist papers as tracing paper, carbon paper and stencil paper, as well as scrap paper for templates and samples. Decorative material can be tracked down in likely and unlikely places. There are many specialist paper shops but you can also find useful materials around the home and much can be recycled from other uses. All decorative paper work must be sealed with varnish for long-term protection. Layers of acrylic varnish are preferable. Apply at least three coats before sanding down to preserve the paper surface.

Printed paper The abundance of printed material provides an invaluable resource for decorative work, principally découpage and paper cut-outs – old prints which can be photocopied, books, magazines and posters, wallpapers and borders are all treasure troves of possibilities. Printed wrapping paper is ideal for découpage or cut-outs since it is often protected by a glossy finish. Other printed matter may well need to be sealed with diluted white craft glue before using. And newsprint is used not only to protect the working area from paint splashes but also to provide the raw material of papier mâché.

Plain paper Even plain papers are now obtainable in a wondrous range of weights, qualities and textures from the lightest gossamer tissue to thick inlaid hand-made papers. Good quality stationery which you can buy in single sheets can provide small samples of exquisite papers that are ideal for decorative work. It is also sometimes possible to buy packets of off-cuts and scraps of paper samples which give ample opportunity for experimenting with colors and finishes. Often even humble packaging material can be given another life in a decorative scheme.

Card Thin card from domestic packaging is useful for trying out paint effects. Use card or corrugated cardboard for papier-mâché molds.

PREPARATION

Decorative paint and paper techniques can be used to renovate old things or to brighten up new ones, but in either case careful preparation makes all the difference to the result. Whether it is to be découpaged, stenciled, or given a special finish such as sponging or ragging, the background surface must be smooth, clean and stable.

Old waxed wood

New bare wood

Varnished wood

Old bare wood

New painted wood

Varnished wood

Old painted wood

Metal

Bare wood

If the wood is new, apply a sealer to knots to prevent resin seeping out. Make sure nails or tacks are hammered well into the surface and fill any holes with wood filler. Remove knobs or handles if possible before applying base coats, but if they are wood prepare these as for the main piece. Prepare the inside of boxes and cupboards as well as the outside.

Sanding down The surface must be well sanded down to smooth off any roughness. If it is very rough, begin with coarser-grade paper and move progressively to fine grade. Wrap the sandpaper around a block of wood for larger flat areas; fold over small pieces once or twice to manipulate them in small or awkward areas or around moldings. Pay particular attention to the edges of doors, drawers and so on. On boxes with well-fitting lids, sand the edges of the lid and box until the lid slips easily on and off – a few coats of paint will tighten up the fit again. Similarly, smooth down the sides and edges of tight-fitting drawers. After sanding, brush well with a soft brush to remove dust and wipe with a clean damp cloth. Allow to dry.

Apply a primer Use a special acrylic wood primer or, if the surface is very uneven, one or more coats of acrylic gesso. Sand down after each coat.

Painted wood

If the surface is in good condition, you need only clean it with a powder cleanser like Ajax or Comet to free the surface of any grease, and then rub it down with sandpaper to provide a proper base for a new coat of paint. If the old paint is cracked and flaking you may need to strip it off completely.

Strip the paint using a chemical paint stripper or hot-air stripper. Work in a well-ventilated area and wear rubber gloves. Scrape off the softened paint in the direction of the wood grain. Finish by rubbing off the residue with steel wool. Wash the stripped wood down well, allow it to dry thoroughly then proceed as for bare wood.

Varnished and waxed wood

Strip old varnish with a chemical stripper. Remove wax with denatured alcohol and steel wool.

Metal

Scrape or rub down metal with a wire brush, steel wool or coarse sandpaper to remove rust spots and paint it with a rust-inhibiting primer. Use oil-based paints for undercoat and top coat.

Terracotta

Terracotta flower pots and troughs make excellent subjects for decorative painting. Scrub used pots first to remove dust and dirt. Allow them to dry. Then dilute white craft glue one to one with water and brush on a coat of the mixture inside and outside the pot or trough. Allow it to dry thoroughly then apply a base coat of white latex as a primer.

Terracotta

THE BASE COAT

If the surface has been properly prepared, the base coat should go on smoothly and evenly. This provides the background canvas which will enhance and display the decorative work.

Tinting latex paint
Small quantities of latex can be tinted with acrylics to whatever color you need.

PREPARING A DESIGN

The motifs and designs used in the projects are provided on pages 134–57. If they are the correct size for the object, photocopy or trace them onto clear acetate or tracing paper directly from the page. Otherwise scale them up or down to a more suitable size.

Resizing the design
The easiest method is to use a photocopying machine. Most modern copiers can resize a motif to between 50% and 200% of the original. To work out the correct percentage, divide the required size by the actual size and multiply the result by 100.

Transferring the design
There are several ways of transferring a design from, for example, copy paper to colored paper or stencil paper. Carbon paper is one of the simplest methods. Alternatively, use a soft pencil to scribble over the back of the design. Turn it over and tape to the stencil (or other) paper. Using a hard pencil or point, retrace the design making an impression on the paper beneath.

Preparing paint and brushes

Use the type of paint specified in the instructions. In most cases this will be latex paint. Give metal objects a base coat of enamel (i.e. oil-based) paint. Latex paint is very easy to apply. Use it directly on top of the primer without an undercoat. To obtain the desired shade you can mix different colors together, or tint paler colors with special color stainers or with acrylic artist's colors. Paint cupboards, boxes and other containers inside as well as out. Paint the bottoms of trays and the backs of frames. Unless otherwise instructed, use the paint undiluted from the can. Stir it thoroughly before applying. Choose a brush size appropriate to the size of the object. Prepare new brushes by washing in hot soapy water to remove loose bristles. Rinse them well and shake vigorously to dry.

Applying the paint

Load the brush to about a third of its depth. Apply the paint in light crisscross strokes. Brush out gently to avoid brushmarks. Allow the first coat to dry thoroughly. Rub down lightly with fine sandpaper to remove nibs, dust particles or loose bristles. Dust off with a soft brush and wipe with a damp lint-free cloth. Allow to dry again and apply one or more additional coats to cover, rubbing down again between coats. Dark colors will require at least two coats.

Using masking tape

Artist's tape can be used to protect areas not to be painted, or to provide a guide for a straight sharp edge when painting panels or stripes. Before sticking down the tape, mark in guidelines with pencil or chalk.
Positioning the tape Lay it in sections close against the penciled guidelines. To prevent paint seeping under the tape, run your fingernail firmly along the edge next to the area to be painted.
Removing the tape Wait until the paint is completely dry, and then pull it slowly and gently away from the painted edge.

FINISHING

It is just as important to pay careful attention to detail in finishing a piece of decorative work as in preparation. Hours of meticulous creative effort can too easily be ruined by heavy-handed shortcuts.

Sealing the surface

Most decorative paint and paper work must be fixed or sealed if it is to last and, in some cases, be durable enough to withstand normal domestic use. Things like trays, chairs and mini-chests need special attention. Other things, such as picture frames, will be handled less. Seal decorated surfaces with varnish – the greater the number of coats the greater the durability. Wax polish can also be applied, instead of or in addition to varnish.

Varnishing

Use the varnish specified in the instructions. In most cases, where the varnish is intended simply to seal and protect the surface, this will be clear acrylic varnish. Unless indicated otherwise, the choice of finish – mat, satin or gloss – is a purely esthetic one and a matter of personal preference.

The surface to be varnished must be completely dry and dust-free. The working area and, as far as possible the atmosphere, should also be dust-free. Allow any final coats of paint or applications of adhesive to dry thoroughly, overnight if necessary.

Sanding down Give the painted surface a final very light sanding with fine sandpaper to remove any dust particles, brushmarks or bristles. Wipe with a damp lint-free cloth and then allow to dry.

Applying the varnish Use an ordinary household paint brush in an appropriate size – ideally, keep it only for varnishing. Alternatively, use a special flat varnish brush. The varnish should be at room temperature to flow smoothly. If it has been stored in a cool place, bring it into the room for about a day before using. Follow the instructions on the container for drying times. Acrylic varnishes are quick-drying – up to an hour depending on temperature and humidity. Load the varnishing brush lightly and apply smoothly but thinly over the surface. Use criss-cross strokes to avoid brushmarks but do not overbrush. Check that the area is completely covered by holding the object at an angle to the light – it is easy to miss patches when using clear varnish. Allow the first coat to dry thoroughly and apply two more coats in a similar way.

Rubbing down Rub down the surface with fine sandpaper after the third coat and between all subsequent coats. After rubbing down, dust the surface and wipe it with a damp cloth. Allow it to dry.

Apply at least three coats to any decorated surface, and as many as seven coats for high durability. Objects which have been decorated with paper cut-outs or découpage may need even more coats of varnish to sink the paper layers into a smooth uniform surface.

Special varnishes

Varnishes can be used as decorative devices as well as for sealing and protecting. Colored varnishes which simulate various types of natural wood are widely obtainable. These can help to mellow a newly painted surface to give it the appearance of age. "Antique pine" and "mahogany" varnishes are particularly effective in this respect. Apply them as the last coat in a series of varnishes. Clear varnish can also be tinted using appropriate colorizers. For tinting clear acrylic varnish, use acrylic artist's colors. Colored varnishes can produce an attractive translucent glow or haze on a decorated surface. Raw umber or burnt umber mixed into clear varnish gives a color which is ideal for instant "ageing." Colored varnishes can also be treated to some of the special paint effects described on pages 50–53. For example, colored varnish can be applied and then ragged off (see page 30), sponged off or combed in the same way as a paint glaze.

Applying colored varnish Use a brush kept only for colored varnish and apply a coat of varnish in the usual way (see above). While it is still wet, wipe off the excess with a clean lint-free cloth.

Tinting clear varnish Squeeze a little acrylic color into a small bowl. Add a little clear acrylic varnish and mix it well into the color. Gradually add more clear varnish until the two are completely amalgamated.

Crackle varnish This specialist varnish produces the fine crazed appearance of the varnish on old pieces of furniture and paintings. It can be used on its own or over other decorative finishes. Detailed instructions are given on page 53.

Waxing

Wax produces a soft, deep, silky sheen which also provides a degree of protection against water and heat damage, although not as much as many layers of varnish. It is available in solid or liquid form and can be applied instead of or on top of a clear or colored varnish. You can also color wax. Mix into the wax a little artist's oil color or shoe polish in the required tone. Apply with a cloth or a brush as appropriate and work it well into the surface. Allow to dry, then buff to a shine with a soft clean duster. Waxed surfaces will need to be replenished from time to time.

Finishes

From top to bottom: colored wax, clear wax, clear gloss varnish, colored varnish, clear mat varnish, tinted varnish. Below: crackle varnish.

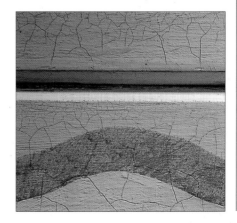

Découpage

*T*he French word découpage means cutting out. It is applied to the practice of decorating things – usually furniture or small objects such as boxes and trays – with cut-out printed paper motifs and patterns. As a craft, découpage is several hundred years old, but it became particularly fashionable during the 18th century when such occupations were thought suitable pastimes for genteel young ladies. At its best, découpage produced exceptionally beautiful results. Traditionally, many layers of varnish were applied to the finished object and patiently sanded down between applications so that the motifs appeared to be inlaid into the surface.

Nowadays modern technology has made découpage much less laborious. Dramatic effects can be produced simply, quickly and with great freshness and spontaneity. There is a wider variety of source material available and photocopying has made it possible to reproduce that material any number of times and to almost any size. Modern glues and varnishes, too, are much pleasanter and easier to handle. They are also quick-drying, which means that you can complete a piece in an afternoon instead of it taking a week or more to finish.

Materials

Motifs Build up a collection of suitable material. Magazines, wrapping paper, fine art posters and postcards, Victorian scraps, old prints and engravings, illustrated books and photographs are excellent sources. Less orthodox sources are sheet music, packaging and advertising material. Black and white images can be left as they are and finished with colored varnish, or they can be photocopied on to colored paper or hand-tinted.

Adhesive The most useful is white craft glue which can also be used diluted as a print sealer. Apply it to large areas with a spatula, to small areas with a fine brush. Use spray adhesive for glueing fine-cut images which might be damaged by too much handling, and for holding motifs in place before sticking them down.

Shellac and spray fixative These can be used instead of white craft glue for sealing prints.

Paint Mat latex paint is most suitable for base coats. Acrylic paints are used for hand-tinting black and white prints.

Varnish Use clear acrylic varnish for sealing and protecting the finish. For greater durability polyurethane varnish can be applied as a final coat. Colored varnishes such as "antique pine" add a mellow antiqued look.

Equipment

Scissors Good sharp scissors are essential. You will need one medium-sized pair for cutting large shapes and one smaller pair for finer work. Manicure scissors with curved blades are ideal for intricate cutting.

Craft knife and cutting mat For even finer work use a craft knife and self-healing cutting mat.

Metal ruler Use with a craft knife and cutting mat for cutting straight lines.

Brushes Apart from brushes for applying base coats you will need brushes for applying adhesive to small cut-outs and for hand-tinting, and larger flat brushes for varnishing.

Roller Use this to roll images flat when sticking them down.

Sponge Use a synthetic sponge or damp cloth to wipe off surplus adhesive before it dries.

CHECKLIST

- A variety of motifs
- White craft glue
- Spray adhesive
- Shellac
- Spray fixative
- Latex paint
- Acrylic paint
- Clear varnish
- Colored varnish
- Medium-sized and small scissors
- Curved manicure scissors
- Craft knife
- Cutting mat
- Metal ruler
- Household paint brushes
- Fine artist's brushes
- Varnish brushes
- Roller
- Synthetic sponge

Découpage techniques

Découpage is basically a very simple craft. There are no complex techniques nor unfamiliar items of equipment to master. But its success depends on taking infinite care with these simple processes at every stage. Surfaces must be prepared well (see page 17) to provide a smooth background on which to découpage. Careful cutting out is vital, as is the patient application of many layers of varnish to the finished work.

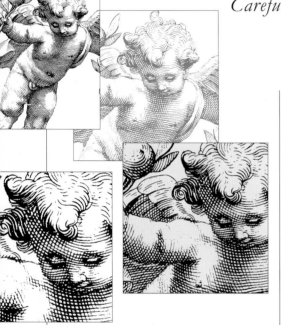

PREPARING IMAGES

Before beginning a project, assemble all your chosen images. It may be necessary to make photocopies or to enlarge or reduce the images to fit the object you are decorating (see left). Photocopy more than you need to allow for mistakes in cutting. Small tears in the paper are not usually a problem as they can be repaired when sticking them down. Black-and-white images can be hand-tinted (see right) or stained to age them artificially (see page 26). You can also enhance or alter the color of existing color images to tone with your design. Add gold or silver highlights or repaint the image as required. Complete all preparation before cutting out.

Images can be enhanced in various ways. In traditional découpage line engravings were often hand-tinted. Use inks or colored pencils or diluted acrylic paints and a fine artist's brush. Seal the images before using.

PHOTOCOPYING

Photocopying has transformed modern découpage. Not only is it now possible to preserve original material but the opportunity to copy an image many times and to enlarge or reduce images at will has greatly added to the versatility and flexibility of the craft.

On most modern photocopiers images can be enlarged (generally by up to 200%) or reduced (generally by down to 50%). To obtain an even greater enlargement it would usually be necessary to enlarge the enlargement, though this often entails a loss of quality and definition.

You can photocopy black-and-white images and color images. You can also photocopy black-and-white line drawings or engravings in color (usually blue or red) and on plain paper or colored paper.

SEALING IMAGES

Avoid discoloration from smudged inks by sealing prints and photocopied or hand-tinted images before cutting out. Use spray fixative, diluted white craft glue (three parts water to one glue), or shellac.

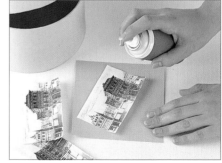

Spray or brush the sealer over the print. Allow to dry. Any creases will be ironed out when the images are stuck down. Sealer also helps stiffen delicate images making them easier to cut out.

CUTTING OUT

Using sharp scissors cut out the images carefully. The most effective cutting method is to keep the scissors in the same position and move the images.

Use a craft knife or scalpel and a cutting mat to cut out intricate details and awkward shapes. Use a metal ruler to cut straight edges. Take great care when handling sharp blades and keep them out of reach of children.

STICKING DOWN

Arrange the cut-out images on the background and move them around until you are happy with the arrangement, using a spray adhesive or glue stick to hold them in place temporarily if required.

On a clean surface apply glue sparingly to the reverse of the images, completely covering the area. For large images use a spatula to apply glue evenly and when sticking down roll them to release air bubbles.

Apply glue to small images using a fine brush or spray. Place the images in position on the background. Press down firmly, moving your fingertips from the center outward to the edges of the image.

Use a damp sponge or clean cloth to wipe off any excess glue from the surface. Allow the images to dry thoroughly before varnishing.

VARNISHING

Seal and protect the images with clear acrylic varnish. Use a clean dry brush that is reserved for varnish. Apply the varnish thinly and allow each coat to dry thoroughly before applying the next one. Apply at least three coats of varnish and seven or more for durability. The more coats you apply, the more the images will sink into the varnish and produce a smooth uniform surface. This is especially important where several images have been layered one on top of another. After the first three or four coats, rub down with fine sandpaper. If required, you can use a final coat of polyurethane varnish on objects, such as trays, which are likely to receive heavier wear.

Use colored acrylic varnishes if required to "age," soften or enhance the color of the object. Apply the colored varnish on top of several layers of clear varnish. For deeper tones use extra coats of colored varnish.

Mini-chests

Plain chests of drawers lend themselves well to decoration. These show how the most basic découpage techniques can produce two very different looks — one for the kitchen, the other for a bedroom.

Antique prints

Old prints are a wonderful source of motifs and with color photocopying you can use them without destroying the originals. Juicy fruits in glowing tones spice up a practical kitchen cabinet; and pairs of cherubs swing gorgeous garlands across a chest just right for glamorous bedrooms.

HARVEST FRUITS

YOU WILL NEED

- ◆ **1 small chest of drawers**
- ◆ **Green and cream latex paint**
- ◆ **Gold acrylic paint**
- ◆ **Fruit motifs**
- ◆ **Craft knife and cutting mat**
- ◆ **White craft glue**
- ◆ **Clear and "antique pine" varnishes**

1 Paint the chest frame green and the drawers alternately gold and cream. Cut out motifs using a craft knife and cutting mat for fine details.

2 When the chest is dry, arrange the fruit motifs on each drawer, either singly or in groups. Glue them down. Allow to dry.

3 Apply at least three coats of clear acrylic varnish, allowing each coat to dry thoroughly before applying the next one.

4 Finish the chest with a coat of "antique pine" acrylic varnish. Brush on the varnish then rub off the excess with a cloth.

FLOWER GARLANDS

YOU WILL NEED

- ◆ **1 small chest of drawers**
- ◆ **Gold acrylic paint**
- ◆ **Pink latex paint**
- ◆ **Cherub and flower motifs**
- ◆ **White craft glue**
- ◆ **Craft knife**
- ◆ **Clear and "antique pine" varnishes**

1 Paint the chest frame gold and the drawers pink. Cut out eight cherubs and enough flowers to cover the width of the drawers.

2 Glue cherubs on each side of pairs of drawers. Glue flower garlands between the cherubs, crossing the join between the drawers.

3 Allow to dry. Using a craft knife, cut through the motifs joining the drawers. Reglue the cut edges. Apply varnishes as for the fruit chest.

Music box

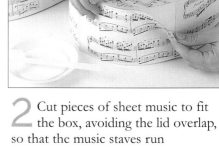

Dramatic découpage effects can be achieved by completely covering accessories with patterned paper and layering motifs on top of that. Gift wrap and wallpaper suggest interesting possibilities or, as here, a covering of sheet music topped with delicate Regency prints of gypsy dancers stained with tea to age them in harmony with much-thumbed melodies.

1 Paint the box cream. Copy the dancer eight times to fit the sides, once for the lid. Dip a tea bag in boiling water. Leave to cool. Press out surplus tea and rub bag over motifs.

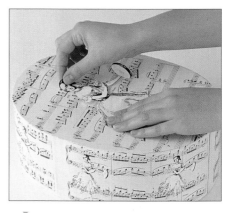

2 Cut pieces of sheet music to fit the box, avoiding the lid overlap, so that the music staves run horizontally round the sides. Glue them down and allow to dry.

3 Using a craft knife, carefully trim the edges of the sheet music closely and neatly around the rim of the box.

4 Cut out the dancers. Glue the large one on top of the box and the others around the sides. Allow to dry. Finish with three coats of varnish.

Tea-ageing
Black-and-white motifs can be artificially aged in several ways. Tea-ageing is the simplest. It produces a gentle yellowy brown tint which perfectly resembles the color of old documents.

YOU WILL NEED
- **1 large oval card box**
- **Cream latex paint**
- **Dancer motifs** *(see page 136)*
- **Tea bag**
- **Large pages of sheet music**
- **White craft glue**
- **Craft knife**
- **Clear acrylic varnish**

Hat boxes

These beautiful boxes are perfect for storing all kinds of precious possessions. The smooth shape is ideal for découpage decoration. Old-fashioned posies, cherubs or kittens - the motifs can be sophisticated or pretty and appealing according to taste.

FLOWERS AND CHERUB

The blowsy blossom and cherub on a creamy rag-rolled background give this box a certain old-fashioned elegance.

YOU WILL NEED

- ◆ 1 large card hat box
- ◆ Cream latex paint
- ◆ Various flower motifs
- ◆ 1 cherub motif
- ◆ White craft glue
- ◆ Colored acrylic varnish in "antique pine"
- ◆ Clear acrylic varnish
- ◆ 4 large brass eyelets
- ◆ Approx 5ft (1.5m) cord and matching tassel

1 Paint the hat box cream. Cut out flower motifs from wrapping paper or magazines. Cut out a cherub motif and enlarge it if necessary.

2 Arrange the cherub and flowers on the box lid and glue down. Arrange more flowers on the side and glue down. Allow motifs to dry.

3 Working on a small area at a time, apply colored acrylic varnish to the lid, then rag off while still wet, as shown on page 51.

4 Apply colored acrylic varnish to the side of the box and rag off as before. Allow the varnish to dry thoroughly.

5 Finish the box with a thin coat of clear acrylic varnish. Allow to dry. Fix eyelets and attach a cord and tassel as shown opposite.

STARS AND CUPIDS

A scattering of silver paper cut-out stars mingle with dancing cupids against a painted black night sky. Two coats of varnish deepen the antique tone.

YOU WILL NEED

- ◆ 1 large card hat box
- ◆ Black latex paint
- ◆ Cupid motifs
- ◆ White craft glue
- ◆ Star templates *(see page 134)*
- ◆ Silver wrapping paper
- ◆ Clear and colored acrylic varnish in "antique pine"
- ◆ 4 large brass eyelets
- ◆ Approx 5ft (1.5m) cord

1 Paint the box black. Arrange cupid motifs on the box lid, side and inside and glue down. Cut out silver stars. Glue them among the cupids.

2 Allow motifs to dry and finish the box with two coats each of clear and colored varnish. Fix eyelets and attach a cord as shown opposite.

CAT AND BOW

*Finish a charming Victorian cat motif
with a stenciled pink bow.*

YOU WILL NEED
- 1 large card hat box
- Blue latex paint
- Cat motif
- Bow stencil *(see page 137)*
- Clear acetate and acetate pen
- Craft knife and cutting mat
- Pink and white acrylic paint
- Masking tape
- Stencil brush
- Clear acrylic varnish
- 4 large brass eyelets
- Approx 5ft (1.5m) cord and
  matching tassel

1 Paint the box blue. Glue the cat
motif onto the box lid. Using the
acetate pen, trace the bow stencil onto
clear acetate. Using the craft knife and
cutting mat, cut out the stencil motif.

2 Tape the pencil in position on
the lid just under the cat's chin.
Using the pink acrylic paint, stencil
the bow. Add white highlights. Allow
to dry. Remove stencil. Stencil another
bow on the side. Allow to dry.

3 Finish with three coats of
clear acrylic varnish.
Fix eyelets and attach a
cord and tassel as
shown at right.

FIXING CORDS AND TASSELS

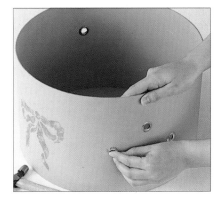

Make the holes Using a bradawl,
make four holes the same size as
the eyelet holes, three in a triangle
on one side and one on the other
side opposite the apex.

Fix the eyelets Use an eyelet to
test the holes for a comfortable fit.
Trim the edges of the holes neatly.
Fix an eyelet in each hole following
the manufacturer's instructions.

Threading the cord Knot one
end of the cord. Thread the other
end from the inside of the box
through the single hole to the
outside. Take the free end over the
top, in through the hole at the apex
of the triangle on the other side,
then out through the second hole
of the triangle and back through the
third hole, threading on tassels as
required. Knot the end of the
cord to secure.

Hat-box trimmings
*Brass eyelets and silky cord
handles give the boxes a
professional finish. The
cords can be bought ready-
made, or you can make
your own from wool, cotton
or silk knitting yarn.
Choose tassels to match the
cords and slip them onto
the cord when threading it
through the eyelets.*

Monochrome

Keep the office or studio neat and tidy with a collection of containers for brushes, pencils and other equipment.

Motifs for découpage turn up in the most unlikely places. These black-and-white borders are designs for traditional wooden moldings taken from an old carpentry manual. Arranged in panels they take on a three-dimensional quality.

YOU WILL NEED
◆ **Variety of containers**
◆ **Cream latex paint**
◆ **Border motifs** *(see page 136)*
◆ **Craft knife and cutting mat**
◆ **White craft glue**
◆ **Fine artist's brush**
◆ **Clear acrylic varnish**

Pencil and paper holders Paint the containers cream. Allow to dry. Copy border designs. Cut them out using a craft knife and cutting mat. Arrange them on the containers, using pencil guidelines if necessary. Glue down, using a fine brush to apply adhesive to small motifs. Allow borders to dry and finish the containers with clear acrylic varnish.

Trompe l'oeil
To enhance further the realistic effect of carved molding motifs, tint them to match the background color of the shelf and containers.

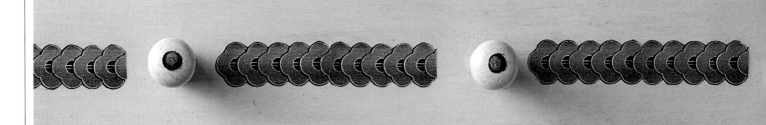

Using varnishes
The look of a piece is much influenced by the type of varnish. Varnishes can be used to "age," distress or add gloss as appropriate. The clear satin finish on the rack is in keeping with its pristine simplicity.

SHELF UNIT

Hang this compact shelf-and-drawer unit on a wall or stand it on a desk top or work surface, so it is conveniently at hand for tucking away all the paraphernalia of a working life.

YOU WILL NEED
- **1 shelf-and-drawer unit**
- **Cream latex paint**
- **Border motifs** *(see page 136)*
- **Craft knife and cutting mat**
- **Metal ruler**
- **Pencil**
- **White craft glue**
- **Fine artist's brush**
- **Clear acrylic varnish**

1 Paint the shelf cream. Allow to dry. Copy the border motifs enough times to fit around the drawer and back of the shelf. Cut them out carefully, using a craft knife, cutting mat and ruler for long straight edges.

SHAKER PEG RACK

The Shakers were a practical people and peg racks were traditionally used to hold everything from chairs to clothing. In Shaker homes the racks would be plain, and this one is very simply decorated.

YOU WILL NEED
- **1 wooden peg rack**
- **Cream latex paint**
- **Border motifs** *(see page 136)*
- **Craft knife and cutting mat**
- **Metal ruler**
- **White craft glue**
- **Fine artist's brush**
- **Clear acrylic varnish**

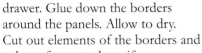

2 Using a pencil, mark out panels on the back of the shelf and drawer. Glue down the borders around the panels. Allow to dry. Cut out elements of the borders and enlarge for central motifs.

3 Piece together the central motifs on the back panel and glue them down in the positions marked previously. Allow them to dry. Finish with at least three coats of clear acrylic varnish.

Peg rack Paint the rack cream. Allow to dry. Copy a border motif enough times to fit between the pegs. Cut out and glue down. Cut out single motifs and glue onto the ends of the pegs. Finish with clear acrylic varnish.

Picture frames

*Frames can be covered with pictures as well as contain them.
Flat wide frames are the most suitable. Decorate them with a pastoral
landscape, or garland them with clusters of grapes and vine leaves.
Hang the frames on the wall with pretty bows made
from two lengths of satin ribbon.*

Variations on a theme
*Landscapes of all kinds –
country, city, exotic locations
– can be built up layer on
layer. Flowers and foliage
would produce a very
different effect from the fruit.*

GRAPES AND VINES

YOU WILL NEED
- **1 flat frame**
- **Masking tape**
- **Dark red latex paint**
- **Ruler**
- **Thin card**
- **Grape and vine-leaf motifs**
- **Shellac**
- **Craft knife and cutting mat**
- **Clear acrylic varnish**

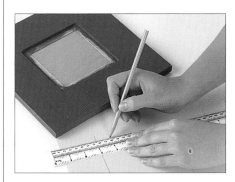

1 Remove the glass or cover it with masking tape. Paint the frame red. Allow to dry. Measure the frame and transfer the shape on to thin card.

2 Paint shellac on motifs to stiffen them. Allow to dry. Cut out grape motifs and glue around the frame shape to overlap central space.

3 Allow motifs to dry. Using a craft knife and cutting mat, cut out the grape motifs. Touch up the edges of the cut-out shapes with red paint to match the frame.

4 Remove masking tape. Position grapes on the frame. Glue down. Allow to dry. Cut out leaf motifs. Glue down on the frame. Allow to dry. Finish with clear acrylic varnish.

RIBBON BOWS

Making the bow Cut two pieces of ribbon about the same length. Take one, fold both ends to the middle and cross them over. Secure with a pin. Place one end of the second ribbon over the cross. Wrap the ribbon twice round to make the knot. Remove the pin and stitch or glue the knot in place.

PASTORAL SCENE

YOU WILL NEED
- **1 flat frame**
- **Background sky and grass pictures**
- **Tree and animal motifs**
- **Blue and green acrylic paint**
- **White craft glue**
- **Clear acrylic varnish**

1 Measure up the frame. Enlarge or reduce the background pictures to cover the frame. Cut out to fit. Cut out tree and animal motifs.

2 Paint the inner edge of the frame to match the sky and grass. Glue down the sky and grass backgrounds. Then glue down the trees and animals, placing the foreground motifs last.

3 Allow the motifs to dry. Finish with at least seven coats of clear varnish to merge the layers into a smooth uniform surface.

Small boxes

Store everything from tapestry wools or jewelry to sweet-smelling soaps in pretty little boxes. They make great gifts, too. Experiment with sizing and coloring motifs, and with different varnishes for an antique finish or one that is fresh and bright.

SCROLL BOX

YOU WILL NEED
- ◆ **1 oblong box**
- ◆ **Mid-pink latex paint**
- ◆ **Scroll motifs** *(see page 135)*
- ◆ **Clear acetate and acetate pen**
- ◆ **Craft knife and cutting mat**
- ◆ **Masking tape**
- ◆ **Dark pink acrylic paint**
- ◆ **Stencil brush**
- ◆ **White craft glue**
- ◆ **Clear and "antique pine" varnishes**

1 Paint the box mid-pink. Allow to dry. Copy scroll motifs three times and the centerpiece twice more. Trace outlines of one set onto clear acetate. Cut out with knife and cutting mat.

2 Mark the final positions of the scroll motifs. Tape the stencils just below and slightly in from these positions. With dark pink paint and stencil brush, fill in the stencil.

3 Allow to dry. Cut out the scroll motifs and glue them in position over the stenciled shadows. Allow them to dry.

4 Apply at least three coats of clear acrylic varnish. Finish with a coat of "antique pine" acrylic varnish. Rub off the excess with a cloth.

Engravings
These elegant scroll and architectural motifs were copied from old engravings and have very much the flavor of traditional découpage. Black-and-white prints can be enhanced by hand-tinting, or add depth with stenciled shadows in a darker shade of the background color.

PIAZZA BOXES

YOU WILL NEED

- **A set of three round boxes in graduated sizes**
- **Blue latex paint**
- **Piazza motifs** *(see page 135)*
- **Acrylic paint in pink, yellow and blue**
- **Spray print adhesive**
- **Craft knife and cutting mat**
- **White craft glue**
- **Clear acrylic varnish**

1 Paint the box blue. Photocopy enough motifs to circle the box, enlarging them to the depth of the box less the lid overlap. Hand-tint with diluted acrylic paints.

2 Allow the box and motifs to dry. Spray the motifs with print fixative to seal the tints. Allow to dry. Cut them out using a craft knife and cutting mat.

3 Glue the motifs around the sides of the box with the street level along the lower edge. Allow to dry. Finish with at least three coats of clear acrylic varnish.

Tea trays

There's no need for objects in everyday use to be dull. Trays, for example, can be decorated with luscious fruit, appealing kittens or a beautiful bouquet. These trays mix découpage with paper cut-outs and have an antique-varnish finish.

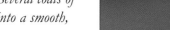

VASE OF FLOWERS

Floral prints arranged in layers in a paper cut-out vase make a beautiful centerpiece for this tray. Several coats of varnish sink the layers into a smooth, practical surface.

YOU WILL NEED
- ◆ 1 wooden tray
- ◆ Green latex paint
- ◆ Flower motifs
- ◆ Vase template *(see page 137)*
- ◆ Chalk or soft white pencil
- ◆ Thick blue paper
- ◆ White craft glue
- ◆ Clear acrylic varnish
- ◆ Acrylic varnish in "antique pine"

1 Paint the tray green. Allow to dry. Cut out flower motifs, including short stems and leaves if possible. Cut out small flowers for corners.

2 Trace the vase template, enlarging it if necessary, and cut out. Using chalk or white pencil, trace around the template onto blue paper. Cut it out.

3 Arrange the vase and flowers on the tray so that some blooms fall over the rim of the vase, building up layers for a rich realistic effect.

4 Glue down the flower motifs that are inside the vase first. Then glue down the cut-out vase so that the rim of the vase overlaps the stems of the flowers.

5 Glue down motifs over the rim. Place trios of small flowers in each corner. Allow to dry. Apply seven coats of clear varnish and one of antique pine.

FRUIT BOWL

A tray decorated with an overflowing bowl of ripe autumnal fruit evokes cosy fireside teas with fruit cake and muffins and plenty of hot buttered toast.

YOU WILL NEED
- ◆ 1 wooden tray
- ◆ Dark red latex paint
- ◆ Fruit motifs
- ◆ Bowl and heart template *(see page 137)*
- ◆ Thick brown paper
- ◆ Pink tissue paper
- ◆ White craft glue
- ◆ Clear acrylic varnish
- ◆ Acrylic varnish in "antique pine"

1 Paint the tray red. Allow to dry. Cut out and arrange fruit motifs. Using the template, cut out a brown bowl. Cut hearts out of pink tissue.

2 Glue down the fruit inside the bowl first, then the remaining fruit and the heart motifs. Cut out corners (see opposite). Glue them down. Varnish as for the flower tray.

CAT AND KITTENS

An irresistible feline family adorns this charming tray. This is a reproduction of an old painting, but you could substitute an enlarged color photograph of your own pampered pets.

YOU WILL NEED
◆ **1 oval wooden tray**
◆ **Pink latex paint**
◆ **Plain paper, for picture template**
◆ **Cat and kittens picture**
◆ **White craft glue**
◆ **Dull gold paper**
◆ **Gold foil paper**
◆ **Clear acrylic varnish**
◆ **Acrylic varnish in "antique pine"**

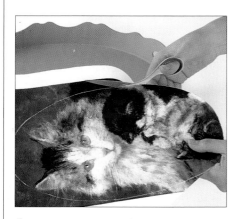

1 Paint tray pink. Allow to dry. Trace tray outline onto paper. Cut it out. Trim off 2in (5cm) all around. Using this as a template, cut out the picture, enlarging it if necessary.

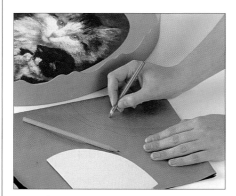

2 Glue the picture onto a tray. Fold template in quarters. Fold the dull gold paper in quarters. Trace folded template on to the folded gold paper, matching corners. Draw a border design to enclose the traced line.

3 Cut out the dull gold border. Glue down around the picture. Make a similar inner border from gold foil paper. Glue it down on top of the dull gold border. Varnish as given for the flower tray.

BORDERS AND CORNERS

Découpage corners A cluster of tiny flowerheads makes a simple corner motif for a flowery tray. For borders repeat small motifs such as these in rows or cut out strips of patterned gift wrap paper and glue them down.

Paper cut-out corners To make a series of simple corner motifs, cut out right-angled triangles of paper. Fold them in half through the right angle and trim the long cut edge in a smooth curve to produce symmetrical shapes.

A choice of borders
These découpage borders have been produced in three quite different ways. One is pieced together from separate cut-out flower and leaf motifs; another is a ready-made border found in a magazine; the third is taken from an old engraving, photocopied and hand-colored with pencils.

Cupboards

Transform ordinary bare cupboards into extraordinary pieces of furniture with découpage and hand-painted decoration. Match the theme to the rooms: those scrumptious strawberries cut from wrapping paper will liven up any kitchen; up in the boys' bedroom the cupboard decorated with drums and drumsticks will prove practical as well as fun.

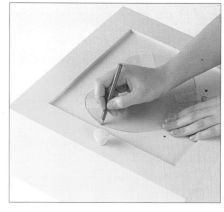

1 Paint the cupboard yellow. Allow to dry. Cut out the heart template. Center on the door panel and mark around it with pencil or chalk.

2 Cut out strawberry motifs. Arrange them around the heart shape and glue down. Glue a fruit in each corner. Allow to dry.

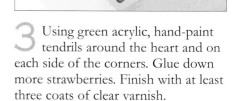

3 Using green acrylic, hand-paint tendrils around the heart and on each side of the corners. Glue down more strawberries. Finish with at least three coats of clear varnish.

WILD STRAWBERRIES

YOU WILL NEED
- 1 wooden cupboard
- Yellow latex paint
- Heart template *(see page 137)* enlarged to fit the door panel
- Colored pencil or chalk
- Strawberry motifs
- White craft glue
- Fine artist's brush
- Green acrylic paint
- Clear acrylic varnish

DRUMS CUPBOARD

YOU WILL NEED

- ◆ 1 small wooden cupboard
- ◆ Latex paint in red, pale blue, blue, green and yellow
- ◆ Drum motifs
- ◆ White craft glue
- ◆ Chalk
- ◆ Brown and white acrylic paint
- ◆ Fine artist's brush
- ◆ Clear acrylic varnish

Drum motifs
Color-copy the drum motifs, enlarging them if necessary, and use acrylic paints to change the colors to fit your scheme if required.

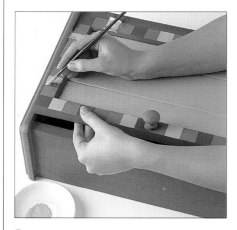

1 Paint the sides, top and door frame red. Paint the door panel pale blue. Add squares of blue, green and yellow to the frame, using masking tape to keep the edges straight if necessary.

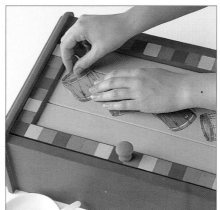

2 Allow to dry. Cut out the drum motifs and arrange them at angles on the cupboard door. Glue them down and allow to dry.

3 Mark the positions for the drumsticks on each side of the drums. Paint them brown with white highlights. Allow to dry. Finish with three coats of varnish.

Carousel toybox

*A large piece of plain furniture, such as this toybox, can be an opportunity
to create an elaborate fantasy. Traditional merry-go-rounds with their gaudy colors
and magnificent painted decoration were the inspiration here. Hunt around for
suitable motifs and photocopy them enough times to provide ample material
for a profusion of centerpieces, repeated borders and corner details.
Touch them up with gold paint for maximum glitter.*

YOU WILL NEED
- 1 large wooden toybox
- Blue and orange latex paint
- Masking tape
- Suitable motifs – fairground horses, carousel poles, borders, scrolls, corners, diamonds, central motifs
- Craft knife and cutting mat
- Gold acrylic paint
- Fine artist's brush
- Low-stick glue
- White craft glue
- Clear acrylic varnish

1 Paint the box blue. Allow to dry. Mark out three panels on the lid and on the front. Mask them with tape and paint orange. Allow to dry. Remove the tape carefully.

2 Assemble all the motifs. Cut out using a craft knife and cutting mat for intricate details. Using a fine brush, touch up motifs with gold acrylic paint as required.

3 Arrange motifs. Place horses and central motifs alternately in the panels, holding temporarily with low-stick glue. Add borders and corners.

4 Glue down the first layer of motifs permanently. Place the poles. Glue down borders to cover pole ends. Then glue central motifs.

5 Glue down the second layer of motifs. Glue down the horses over the carousel poles. Place corner motifs to neaten the panel borders.

6 Finally, glue down the motifs on the back including the central rosette, the diamond border and the scrolls along the top.

7 Allow motifs to dry thoroughly. Apply at least seven coats of clear acrylic varnish, sanding down after the fourth coat.

Child's play

Decorating things for a child's room is great fun. Throw out inhibitions and go for strong vibrant colors and big bold motifs. With découpage you can indulge your nostalgia for childhood fantasies and the timeless appeal of Victorian toys and picture books. Search out scraps and colored prints. Put them together with painted backdrops and finish it with extra coats of varnish to withstand the rough and tumble of nursery life.

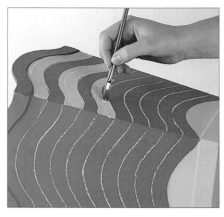

1 Paint the bin blue. Allow to dry. Paint the base yellow, continuing the color on to the sides for the beach. Using chalk to mark parallel guidelines, paint light blue waves on all sides. Allow to dry.

2 Photocopy the boat motifs in red. Cut them out, using a craft knife and cutting mat for the fine detail. Use a spray to apply glue to delicate motifs. Glue them down.

3 Cut out the shell motifs and glue them down on the beach. Allow to dry thoroughly. Finish the bin with at least six coats of clear acrylic varnish.

BOAT BIN

YOU WILL NEED

- 1 storage or waste bin
- Latex paint in blue, yellow and light blue
- Chalk
- Boat motifs
- Craft knife and cutting mat
- White craft glue and spray glue
- Shell motifs
- Clear acrylic varnish

Boat and shell motifs
These line drawings of sailing ships were found in an old book and photocopied in red on white paper. The shells were cut from wrapping paper.

CIRCUS CHAIR

Sheets of reproductions of Victorian scraps are widely available and are ideal for découpage. Apart from clowns, common subjects are cherubs, cats, flowers and children.

YOU WILL NEED
◆ **1 child's wooden chair**
◆ **Yellow latex paint**
◆ **Red and brown acrylic paint**
◆ **Chalk**
◆ **Fine artist's brush**
◆ **Clown motifs**
◆ **White craft glue**
◆ **Clear acrylic varnish**
◆ **Colored wax**

1 Paint the chair yellow. Allow to dry. Using red acrylic paint and a fine brush, paint the front face of the top, two rungs and alternate uprights in the back. Allow to dry.

2 Using chalk guidelines if necessary, continue the red paint onto the seat in curved stripes to resemble parted curtains. Paint the space between them brown.

3 Cut out clowns and arrange them in front of and between the curtains. Trim off parts of the motifs so that they appear to be peeping from behind the curtain.

4 Arrange clown heads on the back of the chair. Glue all the motifs down. Allow them to dry. Apply seven coats of clear varnish. When dry, apply colored wax.

Paint effects

*D*ecorative paint effects fall into two broad categories: broken colorwork and faux finishes. Broken colorwork produces overall textures, often quite subtle and luminous. It includes processes such as sponging, ragging, spattering and stippling. Faux finishes have been used by decorators for centuries to imitate on ordinary walls and surfaces the appearance of more luxurious materials – marble, wood grain and precious metals such as gold and silver. These techniques were often applied on a vast scale – in French cathedrals, English country houses and Italian palazzos – but some of them can also be used on small pieces of furniture and everyday objects in the home.

Modern materials make it easier and quicker to create effects that would once have taken years of careful apprenticeship. The finishes can be used in innumerable ways. They can produce instant throwaway decoration on, for example, wrapping paper or stationery, or elaborate finishes on walls and furniture that will last for years. On smaller objects such as boxes, plant pots, trays and so on, you can go for very simple effects – a plain-sponged, ragged or crackle-glaze finish can look stunning – or something more ambitious. Paint effects make excellent background textures to découpaged or stenciled motifs. You can enhance motifs with gilding, or add gilded borders or finish the entire piece with a fine crackle varnish.

Materials

Paint Traditionally, oil-based paints were used, but nowadays there are water-based products that are equally suitable in most cases and which are easier to use and less toxic. Latex and acrylic paints can be diluted for colorwashing and are available in a wide range of colors. Powder paints can be used to tint latex, and are also used in vinegar-painting.

Glazes For most broken colorwork a little water-based acrylic scumble glaze is mixed with the paint to keep it "open" longer (that is, to slow down drying). Crackle glaze is needed to produce the "peeling-paint" crackle effect.

Varnishes Decorative paint effects are usually sealed with clear varnish. Use water-based acrylic varnish over water-based paints. Polyurethane varnish can be used over water-based or oil-based products. Two-part crackle varnish is used to produce the crazed effect of aged varnish.

Gold size This is a type of varnish which acts as an adhesive to apply metal leaf and metallic powders. It can also be used as a sealer.

Metal leaf and metallic powder For gilding you can use Dutch metal, which is an inexpensive alternative to gold leaf, or metallic powder which comes in a variety of finishes. Wear a mask when using metallic powder.

Paint thinner or denatured alcohol These can be used to create spattered effects.

Acrylic gel medium Mix with powder paints or with metallic powders to produce very effective pigments.

Wax Clear wax furniture polish or plain wax candles are used to distress a paint finish. Wax polish can also be used to seal decorative finishes.

Equipment

Brushes Household paint brushes and artist's brushes are the main requirements. You may also need a special brush for stippling and one for varnishing. Keep one large soft brush or dusting brush for softening and blending brushstrokes. Use stencil brushes for stippling and spattering.

Combing tools Decorator's combs are used for combed effects.

Sponges Use natural sponges for sponging on and off.

Cloths Lint-free cotton cloths are used for ragging. You can also use crumpled paper or plastic bags.

CHECKLIST
- Latex paint
- Acrylic paint
- Powder paint
- Acrylic scumble glaze
- Crackle glaze
- Varnish
- Crackle varnish
- Dutch metal leaf (transfer)
- Metallic powder
- Paint thinner or denatured alcohol
- Acrylic gel medium
- Wax polish or wax candles
- Household paint brushes
- Artist's brushes
- Stipple brush
- Softening brush
- Stencil brush
- Combing tools
- Natural sponge
- Lint-free cotton cloths

Paint-effects techniques

Paint effects range from simple colorwashing to more complex techniques such as gilding and crackle varnish. Most can be used as textured finishes in their own right or as backgrounds for stenciling, découpage or printed motifs. Practice on scrap paper or wood off-cuts before embarking on a project. Experiment with colors, too — close tones are often more successful than strong contrasts.

COLORWASHING

This produces a soft translucent haze of color. Several layers of colorwashing can be built up for a richer, denser result. Different effects can be achieved by varying the brush-work to produce strong, blurred or patchy brushmarks. Colorwashing is applied over a solid base coat in white or another color. Allow the base coat to dry thoroughly before applying the colorwash. Make a latex wash by diluting latex paint with water: one part paint to about three parts water. To make an acrylic wash, mix 50% acrylic paint with 50% water. The paint will be runny so have lots of newspaper covering the working area to mop up the splashes.

Apply the wash to the surface in a random fashion, brushing it in all directions. It can also be applied with a soft cloth or a sponge. While the wash is still wet, use a clean dry brush to brush lightly over the surface, softening the brushmarks if required.

DISTRESSING

The harshness of new furniture or accessories can be softened by distressing the paint finish for an instant aged look. There are several techniques for doing this — some go as far as to simulate fly spots and woodworm holes. Finishes such as crackle glaze and crackle varnish (see page 53) are also designed to produce an artificial antiqued appearance.

One simple effect reproduces the look of wood that has been painted many times, where the top coat has worn to reveal old layers of paint, or bare wood, beneath.

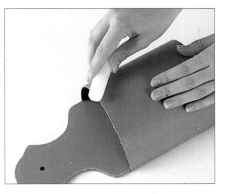

Apply the base coat of latex paint. Allow it to dry. Rub the surface with a wax candle or wax polish. Pay particular attention to areas where the piece would age naturally such as corners, edges, handles, raised moldings and trims. Allow the wax to dry overnight if necessary.

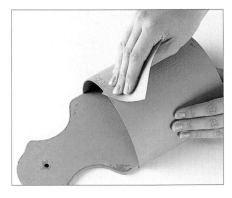

Apply the top coat of latex in another color. Allow it to dry. Rub it down with fine grade sandpaper to remove some of the top coat and expose the base coat. If no additional decoration is required, seal the surface with clear wax and buff with a soft cloth to a deep sheen.

SPONGING

A gentle mottled texture can be produced by sponging paint onto a surface or off it. The effect can be bold or subtle depending on the choice of colors. The best results are obtained by sponging on at least two layers of color. Make a glaze using latex or acrylic paint diluted about one to one with water or mixed with acrylic scumble glaze. Natural sponges are the most suitable. Before sponging on or off, apply an undiluted base coat (the color will show through the sponging) and allow it to dry.

Sponging on Wet the sponge and wring it out until just damp. Dip the sponge lightly in the paint and dab it on scrap paper to test the result and remove excess paint. Dab it gently over the surface, changing the position of the sponge to avoid obvious pattern repeats. Depending on the number of layers, sponge the surface sparingly or closely.

Damp the sponge as before and dip it lightly into the second color. Test on scrap paper and sponge gently over and between the first layer of sponging. Dust with a soft brush as before to blur and merge the colors if required. Allow to dry. Apply further layers of sponging in the same way. If no further decoration is to be applied, seal with several layers of clear acrylic varnish.

While the paint is still wet, you can blur the effect if required by dusting over the surface very lightly with a softening brush. Brush in all directions to blend the paint evenly. Wash the sponge thoroughly and allow the first layer of paint to dry.

Sponging off This technique is useful for irregular surfaces, or for small areas where it might be difficult to sponge on evenly. Wet the sponge and wring out until just damp. Using a brush, apply the diluted second coat on top of the base coat. While still wet, dab the sponge gently over the surface, removing some of the paint and revealing the base coat. Change the position of the sponge often to avoid pattern repeats. Blur with a soft brush as for sponging on if required.

RAGGING

Ragging produces a bolder and coarser texture than sponging. Prepare paint glazes as for sponging and use clean, lint-free cloths. Instead of cloths you can use crumpled paper or plastic bags for a variety of textures. Apply a base coat and allow to dry.

Ragging on Wet the cloth and wring out until just damp. Crumple it into a loose ball, dip lightly into the paint and test the pattern on scrap paper. Dab it gently on the surface, changing the position often. If it becomes clogged with paint, change the cloth. While still wet, dust the surface lightly with a soft brush to blur the pattern if required. Allow to dry. Build up more layers of ragging as required.

Ragging off Apply the paint glaze all over the surface evenly with a brush. While still wet, crumple a dry cloth and dab it lightly over the surface, removing some of the paint. Work over the surface with the rag until a pleasing texture is achieved. Rag-rolling is a variation of ragging off. Form the cloth into a sausage and roll it through the wet paint glaze.

VINEGAR PAINTING

This technique was often used to simulate wood-graining on plain pieces of furniture such as dressers, chests of drawers and trunks, but it is also ideal for creating other patterns and textures. It involves coating a surface with a very simple homemade pigment and impressing objects in the creamy paint to make the design. All sorts of objects can be used for the printing blocks. Try leaves, feathers and molded clay. Prepare the surface by painting on the base coat – the color will show through the top coat. Allow it to dry.

Prepare the pigment In a jug mix together 4 fl oz (125ml) vinegar, 1 teaspoon of sugar and 1 teaspoon of dishwashing liquid. Place a tablespoon of powder paint in a bowl. Add a little of the vinegar mixture to the pigment. Work it into a smooth paste, then gradually add more and mix to a thin creamy consistency. Test the pigment on scrap paper: paint on a layer of the base coat and allow it to dry, then paint on the pigment. Let it dry for a few minutes then try out the printing block. If it is too thick, add more vinegar mixture and try again.

Paint on the pigment evenly over the surface. Work in fairly small areas at a time so that the paint stays workable while you are printing on it. Allow it to dry for a few minutes.

Impress the printing block firmly into the pigment, lifting it cleanly away. Use to create motifs or textures as required. Allow to dry. Finish with three coats of polyurethane varnish.

COMBING

Like vinegar painting, combing originated as a technique to simulate natural wood-graining, but it can also be used to create vibrant geometrical patterns – waves, checks, zigzags and scrolls. In principle it involves drawing the teeth of a combing tool in various ways through a paint glaze, revealing the base coat. Mix a glaze as for sponging (see page 51). Special rubber or metal combs of varying sizes and widths are available, or try ordinary plastic combs, or cut your own from thick card or linoleum tiles. Before combing, apply a base coat and allow it to dry thoroughly.

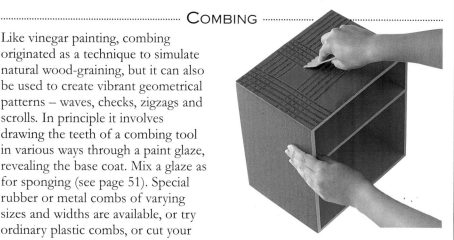

Basic combing Paint a thin coat of paint glaze on top of the base coat. Begin at one edge and draw the comb steadily through the glaze while it is still wet. Repeat across the surface in a regular pattern.

SPATTERING

In this technique paint is flicked onto the surface in small dots sparingly or densely as required. By its nature it produces a very random pattern, although degrees of control can be achieved by using differing spattering implements.

The larger the brush, the larger the spots. For small areas and small dots use a stenciling brush or stiff-bristled toothbrush. For larger areas use a paint brush and a spattering stick. In any loading of the brush the first dots to be spattered will be larger, the later ones smaller. Always test the spatter on scrap paper before spattering the object and dilute the paint if necessary. Allow each layer to dry before applying another one.

To spatter large areas Load a large artist's brush with paint. Hold a long thin piece of wood or another brush (the spatter stick) near the surface and hit the handle of the brush sharply against the stick.

To spatter small areas Dip a small stencil brush or toothbrush into the paint. Holding the brush near the bristles, drag your thumb back against the bristles, flicking droplets of paint onto the surface.

GILDING

Gold or metal leaf and metallic paints and powders can enhance all kinds of decorative work. Nor are they necessarily expensive. One of the most effective gilding products – Dutch metal – is very economical. It is available in small booklets in gold, silver and copper.

Using Dutch metal Transfer Dutch metal is the easiest to use. The leaf is mounted on backing sheets which makes for convenient handling. Gold size is needed to attach the leaf to the surface. Seal porous surfaces with shellac and allow to dry before gilding.

Paint gold size evenly over the area to be gilded. Allow it to become just tacky. Lay the sheets of metal leaf face down on the surface to cover it.

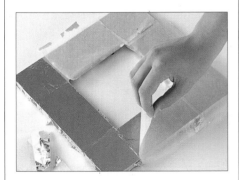

Rub the backing paper gently with your fingers or a soft brush and peel it off. Allow to dry. Clean off loose pieces of leaf. Regild any gaps with scraps of leaf if necessary. Seal with clear acrylic varnish.

Gilding motifs Brush on the gold size in the required shape, through a stencil if necessary. Apply the Dutch metal as described above.

CRACKLE FINISHES

These finishes simulate the look of aged-paint surfaces. There are two quite different effects: crackle glaze and crackle varnish (or craquelure). The first reproduces the peeling of layers of old paint; the second the crazing on the surface of old varnish as, for example, on old oil paintings.

Crackle glaze In this technique a layer of special crackle glaze is sandwiched between two layers of mat latex paint in contrasting colors – the base coat will show through the top coat. The technique itself is simple, but the instructions must be carefully followed for a successful result – it does not always work the first time. Apply the base coat as usual and allow it to dry.

Apply the crackle glaze brushing in the same direction as the base coat. Allow it to dry. Mix the top coat to a thin creamy consistency with water.

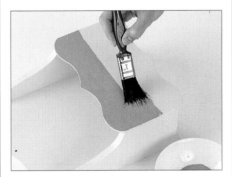

Paint on the top coat with the brushstrokes going in the opposite direction to the crackle glaze. Apply it in single strokes only – do not brush over the area already covered. Cracking should begin almost immediately. A hairdryer will speed up the process. Allow it to dry overnight, then seal with clear acrylic varnish.

Crackle varnish comes in a two-part pack consisting of an oil-based ageing varnish and a water-based cracking varnish. It is the incompatibility between these two which produces the cracks. Seal porous surfaces first with a coat of clear varnish or shellac.

Paint on the ageing varnish smoothly and evenly. Allow it to dry for the time stated on the bottle – this can vary from 1 to 3 hours, but it is also affected by general humidity. It is ready for the next stage when still just tacky.

Paint on the cracking varnish and leave it to dry. The cracks will appear gradually as it dries. A hairdryer will speed up the process and make the cracks more obvious. When dry, the cracks can be emphasized by rubbing a little colored oil paint into them. Wipe off the excess with a clean cloth. Allow the paint to dry thoroughly then finish with a coat of clear oil-based varnish or wax.

Crackle finish

Paint-crackle finishes are excellent backgrounds for other decorative techniques, such as the stenciling on the box and the découpage on the letter rack. Crackle glaze and crackle varnish both produce an antiqued look.

BEETLE LETTER RACK

YOU WILL NEED
- **1 wooden letter rack**
- **Cream and green latex paint**
- **Crackle glaze**
- **Fine artist's brush**
- **Gold acrylic paint**
- **Beetle motifs**
- **White craft glue**
- **Clear acrylic varnish**

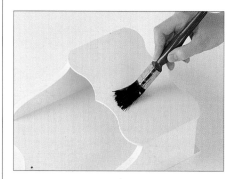

1 Paint the letter rack with cream latex, working the brushstrokes in one direction only (from top to bottom). Allow it to dry. Paint on the crackle glaze in the same direction. Allow it to dry.

2 Using single brush strokes, paint on the green latex in the opposite direction (from side to side). Allow it to dry. As it dries the top layer of paint will slowly crackle, revealing the cream paint underneath.

3 Using a fine brush and gold acrylic paint, paint a fine line around the edges of the box. Allow the gold paint to dry.

4 Cut out beetle motifs and glue them onto the rack as required. Allow to dry and finish with about four layers of clear acrylic varnish.

CELTIC BOX

YOU WILL NEED

- 1 square wooden box
- White latex paint
- Celtic stencils *(see page 138)*
- Clear acetate and acetate pen
- Craft knife and cutting mat
- Masking tape
- Stencil brush
- Acrylic paint in gold
- Two-part crackle varnish
- Green oil paint

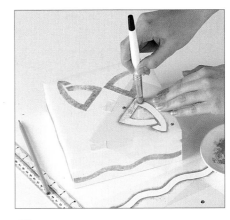

1 Paint the box white. Allow it to dry. Scale up the Celtic design, trace the two main stencils and the border stencil on to acetate using the acetate pen. Cut out the stencils using a craft knife and cutting mat.

2 Tape the border stencil on each side of the box in turn and, using the stencil brush, fill in with gold acrylic. Using gold, fill in stencil A in each corner of the lid, allowing it to dry before removing the stencil. Fill in stencil B on top of stencil A in gold.

3 Allow the stenciling to dry thoroughly. Using a clean dry brush, apply a coat of ageing varnish thinly and evenly over the box.

4 Allow the ageing varnish to dry until it is just tacky (1–3 hours). Paint on a generous coat of crackle varnish. As it dries the crackle effect will appear. Use a hairdryer if necessary to hasten the process.

5 When the box is completely dry, rub a little green oil paint well into the cracks to enhance them. Rub off the excess oil paint and allow the box to dry.

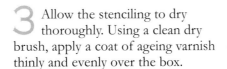

Gift wrap

Use paint effects to create instant original wrappings for special presents. Sponge and stipple gift bags and boxes with background textures. Scatter them with stenciled leafy silhouettes in warm autumnal colors.

GIFT BAG

YOU WILL NEED
- **1 ocher gift bag**
- **Scrap paper**
- **Acrylic paint in dark, medium and pale rust and brown**
- **Natural sponge**
- **Leaf stencil A** *(see page 138)*
- **Clear acetate and acetate pen**
- **Craft knife and cutting mat**

1 Wet the sponge and wring out until just damp. Dip it lightly into dark rust acrylic and sponge gently all over the bag (practice on scrap paper first), altering the position of the sponge occasionally to avoid obvious repeats.

2 Allow the bag to dry. Wash the sponge thoroughly and wring out until just damp. Dip it lightly into medium rust acrylic and sponge gently all over the bag as before. Allow to dry.

3 Wash the sponge, wring it out and sponge the bag very gently again with pale rust acrylic over and between the previous layers of sponging. Allow to dry.

4 Trace the leaf stencil onto acetate and cut out using a craft knife and cutting mat. Using brown acrylic and the sponge, stencil the leaves onto the bag. Allow to dry.

GIFT TAGS

Use the leaf stencils to make matching gift tags. Make positive stencils from the templates, sizing them up or down if necessary. Using a stencil brush and acrylic paint in metallic colors, stipple the shapes onto stiff paper. Allow to dry and cut out. Punch holes and add matching ties.

GIFT BOX

YOU WILL NEED

- ◆ **1 card gift box**
- ◆ **Latex paint in russet**
- ◆ **Leaf stencil B** *(see page 138)*
- ◆ **Stencil paper or stiff paper**
- ◆ **Craft knife and cutting mat**
- ◆ **Bronze metallic powder**
- ◆ **Acrylic gel medium**
- ◆ **Stencil brush**

1 Paint the box inside and out with russet latex. Allow to dry. Trace leaf onto stencil paper. Cut out using a craft knife and cutting mat. Position the stencil on the box lid.

2 Mix the bronze powder with acrylic gel medium. Using the stencil brush, stipple around the stencil with bronze, fading it off toward the edge of the lid.

3 Continue to stipple bronze over the sides of the box, heavily at the corners and edges and fading the color toward the center of each side. Allow to dry.

Ageing gracefully

The technique of distressing gives brand-new accessories and furniture the gently mellow look of age. Add simple potato and sponge prints and these two pretty painted items will add a warm cottagey charm to any modern kitchen.

UTENSIL HOLDER

YOU WILL NEED
- 1 wooden utensil holder
- Brown and ocher latex paint
- White wax candle
- Fine sandpaper

- Large potato
- Felt-tip pen
- Flower template *(page 138)*
- Craft knife

- Blue and red acrylic paint
- Flat plate or tile
- Fine artist's brush
- Clear wax

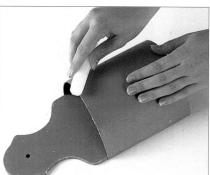

1 Paint the utensil holder brown. Allow it to dry. Rub the cut end of the wax candle firmly along all the edges of the holder. Brush off the excess wax.

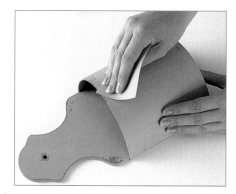

2 Paint on a top coat of ocher. Allow it to dry. Rub the holder all over with fine sandpaper, paying particular attention to the edges, exposing some of the base coat.

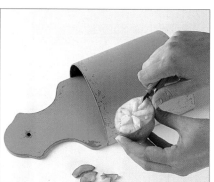

3 Cut the potato in half. Using a felt-tip pen, copy the flower motif on the cut end of one half. Using a craft knife, cut away around the drawing to make a printing block.

4 Mix blue acrylic on a flat plate or tile. Print flowers on the front of the holder. Using a fine brush and red acrylic, handpaint dots for flower centers. Allow to dry. Finish the holder with clear wax.

1 Paint the shelf unit turquoise. Allow to dry. Rub clear wax thinly all over the surface of the shelf using a clean lint-free cloth. Allow it to dry thoroughly. Apply a coat of blue latex over the wax. Allow it to dry thoroughly.

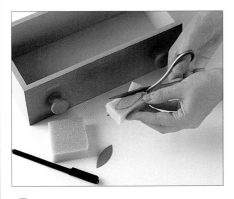

2 Trace the leaf template and cut it out. Using a felt-tip pen, draw around the shape onto the sponge. Cut the shape out of the sponge with a pair of sharp scissors.

KITCHEN SHELF

YOU WILL NEED
- 1 wooden shelf unit
- Latex paint in turquoise and blue
- Clear wax
- Lint-free cloth
- Flat synthetic sponge
- Leaf template
  (see page 138)
- Felt-tip pen
- Sharp scissors
- Yellow acrylic paint
- Flat plate or tile
- Medium and fine sandpaper

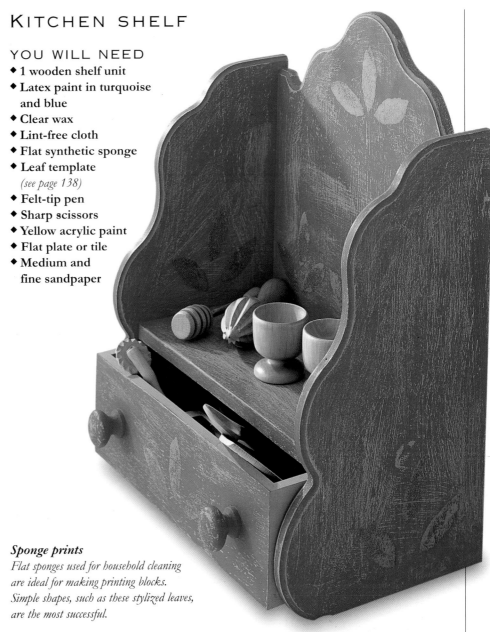

Sponge prints
Flat sponges used for household cleaning are ideal for making printing blocks. Simple shapes, such as these stylized leaves, are the most successful.

3 Mix yellow acrylic paint on a flat plate or tile. Dip the printing block into the paint and print a repeating pattern on the back and sides of the shelf and on the drawer. Allow it to dry.

4 Rub down the shelf all over with medium sandpaper to reveal some of the turquoise paint beneath. Rub down once more with fine sandpaper for a smooth finish.

5 Wipe the shelf down with a damp cloth to remove dust. Allow it to dry. Finish with clear wax and rub all over with a soft cloth for a light sheen.

Metallic matters

*Metal is an interesting surface on which to experiment with different paint finishes.
A verdigris effect makes a decorative object of a plain metal watering can, while
layers of sponging and spattering build up a rich textured surface on the bucket.*

VERDIGRIS WATERING CAN

YOU WILL NEED
- 1 metal watering can
- Metal primer
- Bronze enamel paint
- Fine artist's brush

- Raw umber and metallic-copper acrylic paint
- Latex paint in medium, pale and dark turquoise

- Sponge
- Clear mat acrylic varnish

1 Paint the can inside and out with metal primer. Allow to dry. Paint on a coat of bronze enamel. Allow to dry. Paint the grooves and edges with raw umber acrylic, blending the paint in with your fingers. Allow to dry.

2 Paint on irregular patches of medium and dark turquoise latex, using a damp sponge to blend the two colors at the edges. Allow to dry.

3 Using a sponge, drip diluted pale turquoise all over the can, blending it into the base coat here and there. Allow to dry.

4 Using brush, highlight raised areas, edges and ridges with metallic-copper acrylic, blending it in with your fingers. Allow to dry. Finish with three coats of clear mat varnish.

SPONGED BUCKET

YOU WILL NEED.

- ◆ **1 metal bucket**
- ◆ **Metal primer**
- ◆ **Olive green enamel paint**
- ◆ **Stipple brush**
- ◆ **Acrylic paint in gold, silver, burnt umber and white**
- ◆ **Pale green and dark green latex paint**
- ◆ **Masking tape**
- ◆ **Natural sponge**
- ◆ **Medium artist's brush**
- ◆ **Clear acrylic varnish**

1 Paint the bucket inside and out with metal primer. Allow to dry. Paint on a coat of enamel paint in olive. Allow to dry. Using a stipple brush, stipple gold acrylic lightly all over the bucket. Allow to dry.

2 Mask off the ridge around the bucket. Wet the sponge and wring it out until just damp, then dip it lightly in pale green latex. Test it on scrap paper first, then sponge lightly and evenly all over the bucket. Allow to dry.

3 Wash the sponge thoroughly, wring out until just damp and sponge a layer of dark green latex paint lightly and evenly all over the bucket. Allow to dry. Remove the masking tape.

4 Dilute silver acrylic and, using the medium brush, spatter it all over the bucket. Allow to dry. Repeat first with burnt umber and then with white. Allow to dry. Finish with three coats of clear varnish.

Gilded frames

Objects can be given a glittering finish in many different ways. Paint, powder and metal leaf are easy to apply and give impressive results as is proven by these fabulous frames – grand enough to display precious heirlooms or country treasures.

SPATTERED FRAME

A light spattering of paint thinner on top of colored oil paint gives this plain gilded frame an interesting patinated finish.

YOU WILL NEED

- 1 wooden picture frame
- Brown latex paint
- Gold size
- Transfer Dutch metal leaf in gold
- Artist's oil paint in ultramarine blue
- Paint thinner
- Lint-free cloth
- Fine artist's brush
- Clear polyurethane varnish

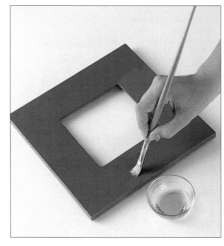

1 Remove the glass and paint the frame brown. Allow to dry. Paint it all over with gold size including the inner and outer edges. Leave until just tacky.

SILVER FRAME

Metal leaf can be laid down in patterns as well as all over a surface. Simply paint the size onto the object wherever you want the metal to go.

YOU WILL NEED

- 1 wooden picture frame
- Red oxide acrylic paint
- Ruler and pencil or chalk
- Gold size
- Transfer Dutch metal leaf in silver
- Fine sandpaper
- Clear polyurethane varnish

2 Lay gold Dutch metal face down all over the frame, overlapping it to cover the surface completely. Rub it down firmly.

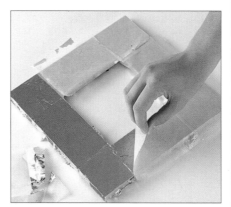

3 Peel off transfer paper. Allow to dry. Clean off loose pieces with a dry cloth. If necessary, touch up bare areas with size and regild. Leave to dry as long as stated on size container.

2 Paint the corners of the frame and alternate stripes with gold size. Leave the size to dry until it is just tacky (touch-dry).

4 Mix ultramarine oil paint with a little paint thinner. Rub over the frame with a cloth. Lay the frame flat. While paint is wet, dip a fine brush in thinner and splash it over the frame.

5 Tilt the frame up and down and from side to side to move the drips around the surface. Allow to dry. Finish with polyurethane varnish.

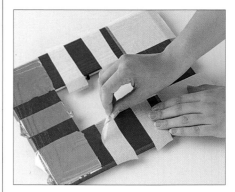

4 Rub the transfer paper with your fingers and peel it off, leaving the metal leaf behind. Leave it to dry. Clean off excess leaf.

MOLDED FRAME

An uneven dusting of silver metallic powder on top of green and copper paint gives this frame a rich bronzed look. The gilding perfectly enhances the sharp ridges of the classic molded frame.

YOU WILL NEED

- **1 molded wooden picture frame**
- **Dark green latex paint**
- **Metallic-copper acrylic paint**
- **Silver metallic powder (and protective mask)**
- **Soft paint brush**
- **Spray adhesive**

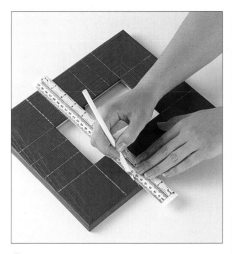

1 Remove the glass and paint the frame with red oxide acrylic. Using a ruler and pencil or chalk, mark off the corners and wide stripes around the frame.

3 Carefully cut the Dutch metal into manageable pieces to fit the stripes and corners. Handling them as little as possible, lay the pieces face down on to the tacky areas.

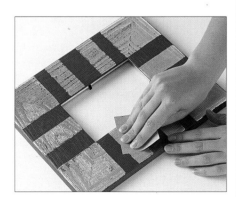

5 Rub all over the frame lightly with fine sandpaper to expose some of the painted surface beneath. Finish with clear varnish or leave unvarnished as required.

1 Remove the glass. Paint the frame dark green. Leave to dry. Paint on a coat of metallic-copper acrylic using streaky brushstrokes, allowing the green paint to show through. Let dry.

2 Using a soft dry brush and mask, lightly dust silver powder all over the frame. Apply the powder more densely over the ridges and in the corners to give them a high sheen.

3 Spray the picture frame all over with spray adhesive to seal the metallic powder. Allow the frame to dry thoroughly.

AGEING GILDED FRAMES

It is very easy to "age" a gilded frame artificially. Rub the frame down with fine sandpaper. Dilute a little raw umber acrylic paint with scumble glaze. Use a small piece of cloth and rub it very thinly all over the frame. Pay special attention to corners and ridges if it is a molded frame, and to any areas of under-coat that have been exposed by the sanding. Allow it to dry. Seal with polyurethane varnish.

Vinegar-painted tray

Vinegar-painting is a very simple technique. It has a direct rustic charm that is very appealing. The pigment is made from materials that are at hand in any domestic kitchen and the patterns are printed with ordinary household objects — anything that will make an impression in the wet paint. Even hand prints and fingers can be called into play. This tray has been printed with corks and shaped pieces of children's clay.

YOU WILL NEED

- 1 wooden tray
- Yellow ocher latex paint
- 4 fl oz (125ml) white malt vinegar
- 1 teaspoon sugar
- 1 teaspoon dishwashing liquid
- 1 tablespoon raw sienna powder paint
- Children's modeling clay
- Bottle cork
- Fine artist's brush
- Green acrylic paint
- Clear polyurethane varnish

1 Paint the tray yellow ocher. Allow to dry. In a jug mix together the vinegar, sugar and dishwashing liquid. Use a little to mix the powder paint to a smooth paste, then add more gradually to make a thin cream.

2 Knead the modeling clay until soft. Mold one piece into a curved shape like a half-moon, and another into a sausage shape about the depth of the tray sides.

3 Paint the vinegar mixture onto the base of the tray. Press the curved shape into the mixture while it is still wet to make flower-like patterns in the center and corners of the tray.

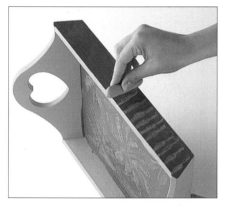

4 Paint one long side of the tray inside and out with the vinegar mixture. Press the sausage shape into the paint to make a regular ridge pattern. Repeat on the other long side.

5 Paint one end of the tray inside and out with the vinegar mixture. Press the end of the bottle cork into the paint to make a pattern of circles. Allow to dry.

6 Using a fine brush, paint the edge of the tray all around and the inside of the handle holes with green acrylic. Allow to dry.

7 When the tray is dry, apply about three coats of clear polyurethane varnish, allowing each coat to dry thoroughly before applying the next one.

Nature's printing blocks
Items such as prettily shaped autumn leaves and feathers collected from the countryside were traditional favorites for making patterns on vinegar-painted objects such as trays and storage chests.

Combed mini-chest

Use combs in different sizes and widths to make a dazzling display of swirling patterns on this brightly colored storage chest. Half-circles, checks, zigzags and waves are just some of the possibilities.

YOU WILL NEED
- 1 wooden mini-chest
- Latex paint in red, yellow and blue
- Acrylic scumble glaze
- Combing tools, or home-made combs
- Scrap paper
- Clear acrylic varnish

Optical effects
Combing was originally used in a subtle way to simulate natural wood grain, but by choosing bright colors and bold geometric patterns it produces a dramatic modern effect reminiscent of the op-art styles of the 1960s.

1 Paint the top, bottom and sides of the mini-chest with red latex. Allow to dry. Paint the inside, the edges of the frame and the drawers inside and out with yellow latex. Allow to dry.

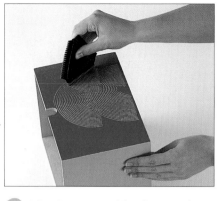

2 Mix three parts blue latex with one part scumble glaze. Paint the glaze onto one of the drawers. While it is still wet, use the combing tool to make semicircular patterns across the drawer (practice on scrap paper first). Allow to dry.

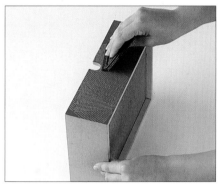

3 Paint the second drawer with the blue glaze. While still wet, use a combing tool to make zigzag patterns across the width of drawer (practice on scrap paper first). Allow to dry.

4 Paint a coat of the blue glaze on the top of the mini-chest. While it is still wet, use a combing tool to make check patterns across the surface (practice on scrap paper first). Allow it to dry.

5 Paint a coat of the blue glaze on one side of the mini-chest. While it is still wet, use a combing tool to make wavy patterns from top to bottom (practice on scrap paper first). Repeat on the other side.

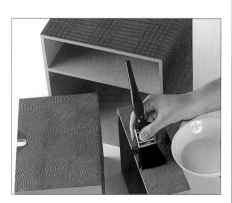

6 Neaten the edges of the drawers and frame with yellow latex if necessary. Allow the mini-chest to dry thoroughly. Finish it with at least three coats of clear acrylic varnish.

Check cupboard

*Dragging can produce a soft, subtle, rather elegant texture or be bold
and colorful as on this vibrant cupboard where strong contrasting tones
are used. The dragging is applied unconventionally in a free
painterly fashion and is lightly distressed while the paint is still tacky.
Cork printing on the check-patterned doors enhances the folk-art effect.*

YOU WILL NEED

- 1 small wooden cupboard
- Latex paint in dark pink, pale pink and maroon
- Lint-free cloth
- Dragging brush (or wide paint brush)
- Narrow paint brush
- Fine artist's brush
- Flat plate or tile
- Bottle cork (or other suitable object for printing circles)
- Clear acrylic varnish

1 Paint the top, bottom, sides and door panel dark pink. Allow to dry. Using a dry narrow paint brush lightly loaded with pale pink paint, drag the door panel in a check pattern. Rub the paint lightly with a cloth to distress it.

2 Using the dragging brush (or wide paint brush) lightly loaded with pale pink paint, drag the top and bottom of the cupboard from left to right and the sides from top to bottom. Allow to dry.

3 Lightly load a dry narrow paint brush with dark pink paint. Drag the frame of the door panel sparingly, working first on the top and bottom and then on the sides of the panel, and crossing the brushstrokes at the corners.

4 Using a fine artist's brush and maroon latex, carefully paint the inner edge of the door frame around the central panel. Allow it to dry.

5 Spread maroon acrylic paint on a flat plate or tile. Using the end of the cork, print circles on the door panel in the squares of the check pattern. Allow it to dry. Finish the cupboard with three coats of clear acrylic varnish.

Printing with corks
Ordinary wine-bottle corks are used to print a pattern of circles over the ventilation holes in the cupboard door. If preferred, these can be omitted, or you can cut an alternative printing block from a sponge or potato using one of the shapes on pages 136-57.

Stenciling

*S*tenciling is one of the oldest methods of decorative painting. Hand-print stencils have even been found in prehistoric cave paintings. Basically, it involves applying color through a cut-out shape (a positive stencil) or around a shape (a negative or reverse stencil). It makes it possible to produce repeating motifs and patterns simply, without the need for advanced painting skills. It is associated most often with folk-art decoration on walls and furniture. In medieval times, the walls of modest dwellings would be stenciled with simple shapes in imitation of the tapestry wall-coverings of more exalted houses. Later, the shapes were applied to paper, then pasted onto walls — the first wallpaper.

Although many sophisticated examples of stenciling can be found — most notably in the products of the Art Nouveau period — its original immediacy and freshness still accounts for much of stenciling's contemporary appeal. But it is a versatile craft. It can be applied to almost any surface — wood, metal, ceramic, paper — provided the surfaces are properly prepared and a suitable color medium is used. It is equally appropriate to covering a large area such as a wall as to something small like a tray or box. The same stencil design can be used in several ways. It can be scaled up or down in size, and the paint can be applied either as one or more flat solid colors, or stippled, spattered or sponged.

Materials

Stencil paper This is thick manila paper soaked in linseed oil. It is strong but easy to cut. Use it for single stencils and for reverse stencils.

Clear acetate For multi-stencils clear acetate is preferable to stencil paper because you can dispense with registration marks. You can trace stencils directly onto it making it very easy to transfer designs.

Carbon paper This is ideal for transferring designs onto stencil paper.

Tracing paper This may also be needed for transferring stencil designs.

Masking tape Attach stencils to the surface with artist's tape. Masking tape is also useful for repairing torn stencils, or for masking off parts of a stencil that you do not want to fill in on a particular project. It can also be used as a stencil in itself.

Double-sided cellophane tape This is used to attach reverse stencils.

Paint Quick-drying acrylic paints are ideal for stenciling. Latex paint is used mainly for background colors.

Varnish Seal and protect the surface with several coats of clear varnish.

Equipment

Acetate pen Use a fine-point permanent black pen to trace stencil designs onto clear acetate. A non-permanent pen will smudge.

Craft knife or scalpel and cutting mat Use these to cut out the stencils accurately from stencil paper or clear acetate.

Metal ruler This is useful for cutting straight lines, and for helping to position stencils on a surface.

Stencil brushes Available in several sizes, these are used to stipple the paint through or around the stencil.

Sponge Paint can also be applied to the stencil with a sponge if a textured finish is required.

Paint brushes Use household brushes for painting background coats and applying varnish. Artist's brushes are useful for adding fine detail.

CHECKLIST
- Stencil paper
- Clear acetate
- Carbon paper
- Tracing paper
- Masking tape (i.e. artist's tape)
- Double-sided cellophane tape
- Acrylic paints
- Emulsion paint
- Clear varnish
- Acetate pen
- Craft knife
- Cutting mat
- Metal ruler
- Stencil brushes
- Sponge
- Paint brushes

Stenciling techniques

Stenciling is an easy way of applying a painted motif to a surface. The design must be transferred to stencil paper or clear acetate and carefully cut out. Color is applied flat or in a textured finish, and can be given depth with highlights and shadows.

PREPARING STENCILS

Templates for the stencil designs used in this chapter can be found on pages 139-51. First scale them up or down to fit the area to be stenciled (see page 18). Then transfer the design onto stencil paper or clear thin acetate. The sheet of acetate or paper should be large enough to transfer the stencil with a wide border of uncut paper or acetate around it.

To transfer the design onto stencil paper, place a sheet of carbon paper ink side down on the stencil paper. Place the stencil design on top. With a sharp pencil, retrace the lines of the design, impressing them through the carbon paper on to the stencil paper beneath.

Transferring multi-stencil designs
Some designs require two or more stencils overlaid one on another. The templates indicate the different areas for each stencil. Trace each stencil separately onto a different sheet of clear acetate.

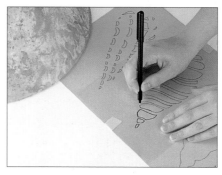

To transfer the design onto clear acetate, simply place the acetate over the design and trace the stencil straight onto the acetate using a fine point acetate or permanent ink pen. Use pieces of masking tape to hold the acetate in position while tracing if necessary.

Registration marks are placed on some multi-layered stencils to help position them accurately on top of each other. Using clear acetate for your stencils helps to eliminate the need for registration marks since it enables you to position stencils accurately by eye. In some instances, however, registration marks may still be necessary. The marks should be traced on each stencil in a sequence, though they need only be cut from the first one. If stencil paper is being used, the registration marks must be cut from every stencil. See page 83 for instructions about how to use registration marks.

CUTTING STENCILS

Using a craft knife or scalpel and a cutting mat, cut around the traced lines carefully. Make smooth cuts around curves. Cut into corners from each side. When cutting multi-stencils, be careful to cut accurately on the line for a neat fit.

ATTACHING STENCILS

Stencils must be closely attached to the surface to avoid paint seeping under the edges. Trim the edges of the stencil to help it lie flat around protruding features such as handles or moldings. With quick-drying acrylic paint, it is enough to hold the stencil with masking tape. Hold your fingers near the cut edge when stippling to help keep contact with the surface.

APPLYING PAINT

Paint can be applied in a number of ways. The most common are with a stencil brush or a sponge.

Using a stencil brush Dab a little paint onto the brush. Test it on scrap paper to ensure that the brush is not too heavily loaded. Holding the brush at 90° to the surface, stipple on the paint lightly all over the shape, going over the stencil at the cut edges to ensure a firm line. Allow to dry before removing the stencil.

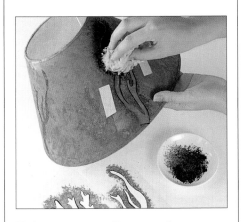

Using a sponge Dampen the sponge and wring out excess water. Dip into the paint and test on scrap paper. Dab gently all over the shape. Allow to dry before removing the stencil.

Other techniques Color can be applied to stencils, or reverse stencils, in other ways. Some of the paint finishes described on pages 50-53 would be suitable. Ragging and spattering can be very effective. You can also gild through a stencil. Paint gold size through the stencil instead of color. Allow to dry, remove the stencil and apply metal leaf as usual.

ADDING HIGHLIGHTS AND LOWLIGHTS

Some stencil designs depend on areas of flat color for their effectiveness. Others can be given depth with highlights and shadows stenciled at the same time as the main color.

Adding highlights Stencil on the main color. On the same palette mix a little white acrylic into the main color and dab it down the other side of the shape along the outer edge, blending it into the main color.

Adding lowlights Stencil on the main color. Add highlights if required. Then on the same palette mix a little black or raw umber into the main color and dab it down the other side of the shape along the outer edge, blending it into the main color.

REPEAT PATTERN BORDERS

Border stencils are usually supplied as a repeat pattern. Stencil one repeat in the usual way, then lift the stencil, move it along the border area and stencil again, continuing in this way until the border is complete. It is important to align the repeats accurately. On some designs there will be a registration mark. Alternatively, where the pattern is a regular one, you can overlap the first few motifs of subsequent repeats over the last few motifs of the previous one.

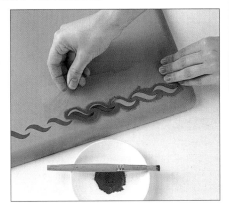

REVERSE STENCILING

Reverse, or negative, stenciling is where the paint is applied around a shape rather than through it. Any cut-out image or outline can be used as a reverse stencil.

Attach the shape or shapes to the surface with spray adhesive or double-sided cellophane tape applied to the back. Using any appropriate method, apply paint to the surface well over and around the edges of the stencil. Allow to dry and remove the stencil.

Stationery set

Use classic-scroll stencils to create a coordinated set of original stationery and decorate a matching rack to hold it. You can apply the stencils in various ways, at different angles, reversing them, masking off parts and so on.

SCROLL LETTER RACK

YOU WILL NEED
- **1 wooden letter rack**
- **Pale blue latex paint**
- **Clear acetate and acetate pen**
- **Scroll stencils** *(see page 139)*
- **Craft knife and cutting mat**
- **Masking tape**
- **Stencil brush**
- **Red and brown acrylic paint**

STATIONERY

YOU WILL NEED
- **Heavy blue notepaper and envelopes**
- **Scroll stencils used for letter rack**
- **Pale blue and red acrylic paints**
- **Stencil brush**
- **Spray adhesive**

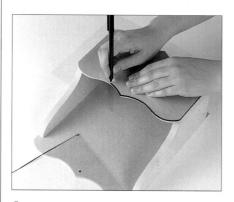

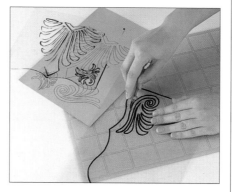

1 Paint the letter rack pale blue. Trace around the back and front of the rack onto acetate and cut out to make two templates. Scale up the three scroll designs to fit the templates.

2 Trace them in position onto the acetate templates for the front and back, reversing them where necessary. Cut out using a craft knife and cutting mat.

Watermarks Use any of the scroll stencils and pale blue acrylic to stipple a design lightly on the notepaper. Allow to dry. Finish with spray adhesive.

3 Tape the back stencil in position. Using the stencil brush, fill in with red. Allow to dry, then stencil shadows in brown. Allow to dry and remove stencil.

4 Tape the front stencil in place. Using the stencil brush, fill in with red. Allow to dry, then stencil shadows in brown. Allow to dry. Finish with clear varnish.

Corner motifs Use parts of stencils, masking off the rest, to stencil small motifs in the corners of envelopes and notepaper.

Farmyard mini-chest

Any shape can be used as a reverse stencil as long as it is recognizable in silhouette. These animal shapes, taken from an old children's game, fit the bill perfectly. The idea can be easily translated into other contexts. Flower shapes, for example, would look good on a bedroom mini-chest, and vegetable shapes on one meant for the kitchen.

YOU WILL NEED
- 1 wooden mini-chest
- Acrylic paint in medium and dark blue, pink, yellow, orange, green and red
- Animal templates *(see page 140-1)*
- Stiff paper or stencil paper
- Double-sided cellophane tape
- Stencil brush
- Brown latex paint
- Fine artist's brush
- Clear acrylic varnish

Farmyard characters

There are 11 animal templates on pages 140–1. Choose your favorite ones to stencil onto the drawers of the mini-chest.

1 Colorwash the front of the drawers using diluted acrylic paint in medium blue, dark blue, pink, yellow and orange.

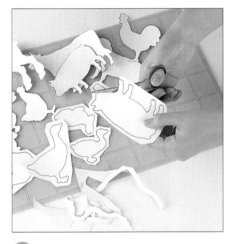

2 Photocopy or trace the animal templates onto stiff paper or stencil paper, enlarging them to fit the drawers. Cut them out carefully.

3 Using double-sided cellophane tape, fix templates on drawers. Using green acrylic, stipple around templates and over drawers.

4 Colorwash the top of the chest in orange and the sides in pink. Fix your chosen animal templates in position as before. Stipple around them with green acrylic paint.

5 Allow the chest to dry and remove the templates. Paint the front frame and drawer edges brown. Using a fine brush and red acrylic, paint a zigzag line on the front frame.

6 Allow the chest to dry. Apply at least three coats of clear acrylic varnish, allowing each coat to dry before applying the next one.

Canal cans

Make gardening indoors or out even more pleasurable with this cheerful collection of cans. The colorful naive style is reminiscent of traditional painted items on the narrow boats that ply the English waterways.

FRUITY BUCKET

Bring the harvest home in a bright painted bucket stenciled with sprays of glowing autumnal fruit.

YOU WILL NEED
- 1 metal bucket
- Orange enamel paint
- Fruit stencils *(see page 142)*
- Carbon paper
- Stencil paper
- Craft knife and cutting mat
- Double-sided cellophane tape and masking tape
- Acrylic paint in white, yellow ocher, red, green, brown and blue
- Fine artist's brush
- Clear polyurethane varnish

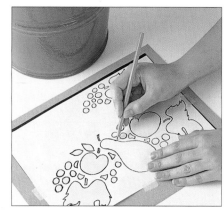

1 Paint the bucket inside and out with orange enamel. Allow to dry. Scale up the stencils to fit the bucket and, using carbon paper, transfer them to stencil paper.

2 Using a craft knife and cutting mat, cut out the stencils. Trim them to lie flat on the bucket. Secure with double-sided cellophane tape and masking tape.

3 Using yellow ocher acrylic and white, stencil highlights on the top edge of all the shapes, then yellow ocher on the pears and red on the peaches.

4 Finish stenciling the pears, grapes and leaves with green. Stencil the stems with brown. Allow to dry. Remove the stencils.

5 Using a fine brush, paint a blue border following the existing grooves of the can. Allow to dry. Varnish with seven coats of clear polyurethane over the stenciled areas.

WATERING CAN

These stylized flowers and scroll borders echo traditional bargee decoration.

YOU WILL NEED
- 1 metal watering can
- Enamel paint in green, red and yellow
- Fine artist's brush
- Flower, petal, leaf and scroll stencils *(see page 143)*
- Clear acetate and acetate pen
- Craft knife and cutting mat
- Masking tape
- Acrylic paint in cream, yellow, pink, red, white and green
- Stencil brush
- Clear polyurethane varnish

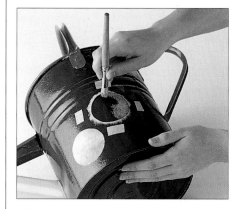

2 Tape the flower stencil to the can. Using a stencil brush and blending cream, yellow and pink acrylic, stencil three flowers on each side of the can. Allow to dry.

4 Tape the leaf stencils onto the can around the flowers as required. Using green acrylic, stencil the leaves, adding highlights along the edge of each one.

PLANT CONTAINER

Four stencils are used for a multi-colored feathery motif which is repeated all around the container.

YOU WILL NEED
- 1 metal plant container
- Brown enamel paint
- Feather stencils *(see page 143)*
- Clear acetate and acetate pen
- Craft knife and cutting mat
- Masking tape
- Acrylic paint in yellow ocher, orange, green and cream
- Stencil brush
- Clear polyurethane varnish

1 Paint the can inside and out with green enamel. Using enamel, paint top and spout yellow, the handles red with yellow edges. Scale up stencils, trace onto acetate and cut out.

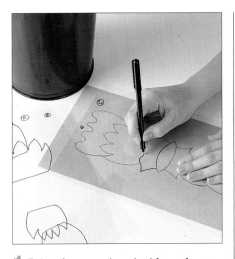

1 Paint the container inside and out with brown enamel. Scale up the stencils. Trace onto acetate including registration marks. Cut out, using a craft knife and cutting mat.

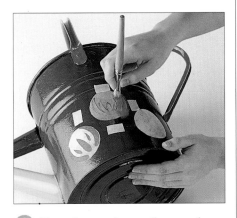

3 Tape the petal stencils over the flowers as required. Using red acrylic, stencil the petals on top of the basic flower shapes. Allow to dry.

2 Tape stencil A in place. Using ocher, stencil outer edges of motifs. Allow to dry. Repeat around the can. Repeat with stencil B using orange, matching registration marks.

3 Allow to dry. Repeat the process with stencil C using green acrylic. Allow to dry and repeat with stencil D using cream acrylic and stenciling the shape solid.

5 Tape the scroll stencil between the grooves around the can. Using cream acrylic, stencil the border, moving the stencil as the paint dries. Finish the can as for the bucket.

4 Using the top part of stencil C and green, stencil a repeat pattern border around the top edge of the can. Allow to dry and finish as for the bucket.

REGISTRATION MARKS

Where stencils are overlaid on each other, they must be aligned correctly. With acetate stencils this is often done by eye, but sometimes registration marks are needed. These are marked on the template. Trace the mark onto each stencil. When cutting the first stencil, cut small holes at the marked points. Position first stencil. Chalk onto the surface through the hole. Align registration marks over the chalk marks on subsequent stencils.

Lampshades

Shed new light on your surroundings with a pair of lampshades with an aquatic theme. The shades have three layers of stenciling and ragged-on backgrounds, using two colors on the sea-shell shade and three on the aquarium shade.

SEA-SHELL SHADE

YOU WILL NEED
- 1 plain lampshade
- Ocher and rust latex paint
- Clean lint-free cloth, for ragging
- Shell stencils *(see page 144)*
- Clear acetate and acetate pen
- Craft knife and cutting mat
- Masking tape
- Stencil brush
- Acrylic paint in brown, pink and red
- Clear acrylic varnish

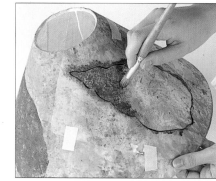

1 Colorwash shade, using diluted latex in ocher (see page 50). Using the cloth, rag on a layer of rust (see page 51). Scale up shell design, trace stencils onto acetate and cut out, using craft knife and cutting mat.

2 Tape stencil A in position at an angle on the shade. Using a stencil brush and brown acrylic, fill in the stencil. Allow to dry, remove the stencil, and repeat twice more evenly spaced around the shade.

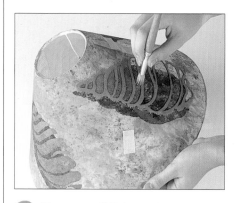

3 Tape stencil B in position slightly to the right of stencil A. Using the stencil brush, fill in with pink. Allow to dry. Remove stencil.

4 Tape stencil C in position. Using stencil brush, fill in with red. Allow to dry. Remove stencil. Finish with clear acrylic varnish.

AQUARIUM SHADE

YOU WILL NEED
- 1 plain lampshade
- Latex paint in pale green, mid-green and blue
- Clean lint-free cloth, for ragging
- Aquarium stencils *(see page 144)*
- Clear acetate and acetate pen
- Craft knife and cutting mat
- Masking tape
- Acrylic paint in green, pink, yellow, purple, orange, brown and red
- Small natural sponge
- Clear acrylic varnish

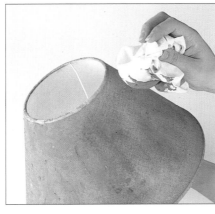

1 Colorwash the shade, using diluted latex paint in pale green (see page 50). Allow to dry. Colorwash again using diluted mid-green latex. Allow to dry. Using the cloth, rag on a layer of blue latex (see page 51).

2 Scale up the aquarium stencils and trace them onto acetate using the acetate pen. Cut the images out carefully using the craft knife and cutting mat – you will have four seaweed and six fish stencils (one main stencil and one stripe stencil for each fish).

3 Position the seaweed stencils, holding with masking tape. Using acrylic paint in green and pink, fill in lightly with a damp sponge. Allow to dry. Repeat stencils around the shade as required.

4 Position main fish stencils and sponge with yellow, purple and orange. When dry, stencil on stripes in brown, orange and red. Allow to dry. Finish with clear acrylic varnish.

Banner tray

Serve morning coffee and cream cakes on this elegant oval tray. The simple double stencil is enhanced with lots of added highlights and shadows to create a fluttering banner. Small banners also decorate the outside of the tray's prettily scalloped edge.

YOU WILL NEED
- 1 oval wooden tray
- Beige latex paint
- Clear acetate and acetate pen
- Banner stencils *(see page 145)*
- Craft knife and cutting mat
- Masking tape
- Stencil brush
- White and burnt umber acrylic paint
- Clear acrylic varnish
- Clear wax

Alternative designs
Banner designs are easily translated into stencils. Simplify them into component shapes. Put areas that are mostly light on one stencil and areas that are mostly dark on another. Letter stencils are widely available. Use them to stencil an appropriate slogan or message.

Bon appétit

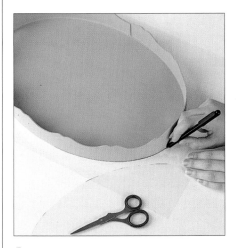

1 Paint the tray beige. Trace around it onto acetate to make a template. Cut out the template just inside the traced line to fit the tray neatly. Make a second template in a similar way.

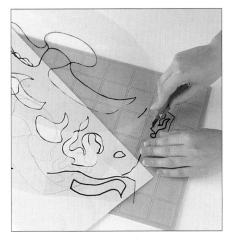

2 Scale up main banner design and trace the two stencils onto the acetate templates. Cut them out, using a craft knife and cutting mat. Scale up the small banner to fit the edge. Trace and cut out the two stencils as usual.

3 Position stencil A. Using a stencil brush, fill in with burnt umber acrylic. Allow to dry. Remove stencil. Position stencil B. Fill in with white acrylic. Position and stencil a small banner inside the tray similarly.

4 Replace stencil A. Using burnt umber mixed with a little white, stencil in highlights. Allow to dry. Remove stencil. Replace stencil B. Stencil in shadows using white mixed with a little burnt umber. Repeat for the small banner.

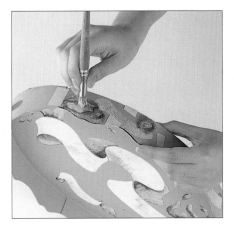

5 Stencil four small banners around the outside edge of the tray in a similar way, stenciling the main colors first, then filling in the highlights and shadows.

6 When the tray is dry, apply at least seven coats of clear acrylic varnish, allowing each coat to dry thoroughly before applying the next one. Finally, apply clear wax with a clean cloth.

Square boxes

Plain boxes provide plenty of scope for decoration. These two, which house a connoisseur's collection of ties and bow ties, have been treated to a burst of jazzy geometrics. You can paint the insides of the boxes in toning colors or line them with paper.

TARTAN TIE BOX

This pattern of stripes overlaid one on another by the cunning use of masking-tape stencils, closely resembles the natural woven look of real woolen tartans.

YOU WILL NEED
- 1 square wooden box
- Green latex paint
- **Tartan template** *(see page 145)*
- Pencil marker
- Masking tape
- Stencil brush
- Acrylic paint in red, yellow, brown and blue
- Clear acrylic varnish

1 Paint the box green. Starting in a corner of the lid, place the tartan template along the edge of the box and mark off the stripe positions with a pencil. Repeat around the lid.

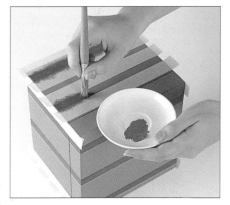

2 Mask off stripes A on the lid, continuing them down two sides. Using red acrylic, stencil in stripes A. Allow to dry. Remove tape. Using the template, mark tartan pattern on the other two sides. Stencil stripes A.

3 Mask off stripes B on the lid and continue down two sides. Stencil stripes B in yellow, stippling lightly to simulate woven tartan. Allow to dry. Remove tape. Mask off and stencil stripes B along the other two sides.

4 Continuing as set, stencil stripes C, D and E in brown, blue and brown (lightly) respectively. Allow all colors to dry and remove tape before applying the next one. Finish with four coats of clear varnish.

Scottish tartans
There are many authentic Scottish tartan patterns covering a huge range of colorways from bright to somber. The tartan template can be recolored to resemble the overall feeling of any of these plaids.

ALTERNATIVE COLORWAYS

Geometric patterns lend themselves to endless experimentation with colorways. With tartan you have the real thing to study for reference. Try matching the colors of a genuine Scottish family tartan such as the examples shown below. The bow-tie design calls for a wilder touch — the more electric the colors the better. You can also use the border stencils to add extra stripes on each side, giving you even more scope for vibrant optical effects.

Pink colorway
This alternative is a fantasy tartan with shocking pink as the main color.

BOW-TIE GEOMETRICS

A collection of natty bow ties deserves a beautiful storage box. This stenciled pattern tells you exactly what is inside.

YOU WILL NEED
- ◆ **1 square wooden box**
- ◆ **Blue latex paint**
- ◆ **Bow-tie stencils** *(see page 145)*
- ◆ **Clear acetate and acetate pen**
- ◆ **Craft knife and cutting mat**
- ◆ **Chalk**
- ◆ **Masking tape**
- ◆ **Stencil brush**
- ◆ **Rust and gold acrylic paint**
- ◆ **Clear acrylic varnish**

1 Paint the box blue. Scale up the stencils, trace onto acetate and cut out with craft knife and cutting mat. Chalk position guides on lid and sides.

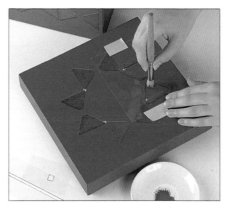

2 Tape the main bow stencil in position and, using rust acrylic, stencil two rows of bows on each side of the box. Stencil four bows in square formation on the lid.

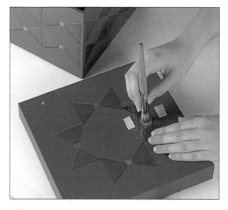

3 Tape knot stencil in position on the first bow, marking the bow corners on stencil with acetate pen as a position guide for remaining bows. Using gold, stencil the bow knots.

4 Tape border stencil across one side of first bow and tape along edges of bow to create a bow-stripe stencil. Stencil stripes in gold on all bows, reversing stencil for the second sides. Stencil gold borders around lid. Finish with four coats of varnish.

Flower pots

Transform terracotta pots or planters with a coat of paint and stenciled motifs.
Provided they are sealed first with diluted white adhesive the paint surface is durable.
They will grace any window sill or conservatory, although they are not suitable for outdoors.
Plants should be potted up in plastic liner pots before being put into them.

TRAILING IVY TROUGH

YOU WILL NEED
- 1 terracotta plant trough
- Cream and pink latex paint
- Masking tape
- Ivy stencils *(see page 147)*
- Clear acetate and acetate pen
- Craft knife and cutting mat
- Stencil brush
- Dark green and light green acrylic paint
- Fine artist's brush
- Clear acrylic varnish

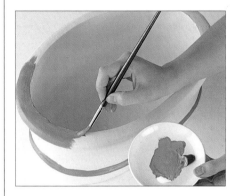

1 Paint the trough cream. Using masking tape, paint the upper and lower ridges pink. Scale up the stencil, trace onto acetate and cut out using a craft knife and cutting mat.

2 Tape the stencil in position on the trough so that the leaves fall on both sides of the ridge. Using a stencil brush, fill in with dark green. Allow to dry. Remove stencil and repeat around the pot.

3 Replace stencil. Holding a card to shield the background, use a stencil brush and diluted light green paint to spatter on top of the leaves. Allow to dry. Repeat around trough.

4 Using a fine brush, dark green paint and light green for high-lights, hand-paint tendrils and stems to join the leaves. Allow to dry. Finish with six coats of clear varnish.

SWAG POT

YOU WILL NEED

- 1 terracotta flower pot
- Latex paint in pale yellow, dark yellow and blue
- Masking tape
- Mid-blue and pale blue acrylic paint
- String
- Swag stencils *(see page 146)*
- Clear acetate and acetate pen
- Craft knife and cutting mat
- Stencil brush
- Clear acrylic varnish

1 Paint the pot pale yellow inside and out. Allow to dry. Mask borders top and bottom. Paint with dark yellow latex. Allow to dry. Paint two inner borders similarly in mid-blue.

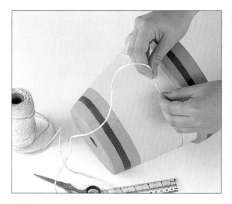

2 Using a length of string, measure around the pot just below the ridge. Divide this measurement into four. Scale up the swag design to fit one of these quarters. Trace the two stencils onto acetate and cut them out carefully using a craft knife and cutting mat.

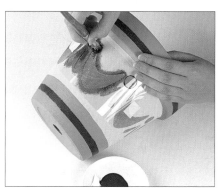

3 Tape stencil A on the pot. Stencil with pale blue acrylic. Allow to dry, remove stencil and repeat three more times, overlapping knots to align stencil. Repeat stencil A again using mid-blue for shadows.

4 Tape stencil B in position on top of the swag and fill in with mid-blue. Allow to dry. Remove the stencil. Finish with six coats of clear acrylic varnish.

Tulip chair

Plain wooden furniture is a traditional vehicle for stenciling especially in European folk-art decoration. Fruit and flowers are favorite motifs, and they range from very simple and stylized, as here, to subtle complex compositions featuring careful blending of colors and tones. This chair with its distressed background finish and bright fresh blues, greens and pinks is inspired by Scandinavian painted furniture.

YOU WILL NEED

- **1 wooden chair**
- **White and blue latex paint**
- **Tulip stencils** *(see page 146)*
- **Clear acetate and acetate pen**
- **Craft knife and cutting mat**
- **Chalk**
- **Masking tape**
- **Acrylic paint in green, light green, pink and dark pink**
- **Stencil brush**
- **Clear acrylic varnish**

Paint finishes

Decorative paint effects provide an attractive background for stenciling. The tulip chair has a distressed-paint finish, which is described in detail on page 50. Colorwashing, sponging and ragging are alternative treatments and instructions for producing these finishes can be found on pages 50–51.

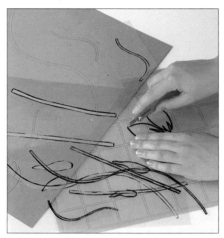

1 Paint the chair white. Allow to dry. Paint it blue and distress the finish (see page 50). Scale up and trace the tulip stencils on to acetate. Cut out using a craft knife and cutting mat.

2 Arrange the wavy stem stencil on the seat and mark the final position of the two crossed central stems, chalking through the cut stencil.

3 Using green acrylic with light green for highlights, stencil the stems on the seat. Stencil leaves along the stems in the same way. Allow the paint to dry between stencilings.

4 Stencil two tulip petals in pink at the end of each stem. Stencil two additional petals in dark pink slightly offset from the first two.

5 Stencil straight stems and leaves in two greens as before on the chair back. Stencil a tulip in pink and dark pink on the cross-bar.

6 Stencil leaves and a tulip on the front face of the seat. Allow all stencils to dry. Apply at least four coats of clear acrylic varnish.

Sports chest

Keep all your cumbersome sports equipment in this sturdy, capacious storage box. It's just the right size for racquets, balls and boots — all the necessities of an energetic sporting life. The stenciled pictures on the sides and lid may look complicated but are actually very simple to do. Many pictures could be given the same treatment, and the chest adapted to different uses — a toybox, for example.

Mixed doubles
The sporting scene is stenciled on the top of the chest and reversed on the front of the chest. The reversed image is achieved simply by turning the stencils over and stenciling from the other side. Clean the front of the stencils before reversing them.

YOU WILL NEED

- 1 wooden blanket box
- Masking tape
- Cream latex paint
- Net stencil (see page 151)
- Picture stencils (see pages 148-9)
- Clear acetate and acetate pen
- Craft knife and cutting mat
- Natural sponge
- Stencil brush
- Acrylic paint in blue, turquoise, flesh, green, light green, red, yellow, brown, mint green
- Clear wax

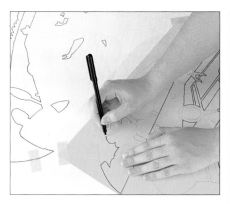

1 Mask off a panel on the lid and front for the picture. Paint the panels cream. Scale up the net stencil, trace onto acetate, and cut out, using a craft knife and cutting mat. Sponge the net pattern on each side of the picture panels using cream latex.

2 Scale up the picture stencil to fit the panel. Mark the oval outline on the picture panels. Following the shapes indicated for stage one, trace the first stencil onto acetate. In a similar way make stencils for stages two, three and four.

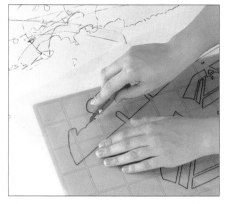

3 Using a craft knife and cutting mat, cut out the four stencils very carefully, making sure to cut exactly on the line so that the stencils fit together precisely.

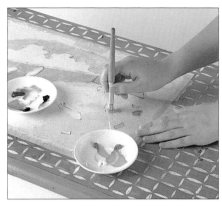

4 Tape first stencil in place inside picture outline. Using the stencil brush, stencil the sky in blue, high netting in turquoise and skin tones in flesh. Allow to dry. Remove stencil.

5 Tape second stencil in place. Stencil trees in green and rust, court in light green, skin tones in flesh. Stipple red and yellow on to trees. Allow to dry. Remove stencil.

6 Tape the third stencil in place. Stencil the tree trunks, hair and net posts in brown, ball in white, shorts and racquet bands in red, racquet strings in grey and skin in flesh. Allow to dry. Remove stencil.

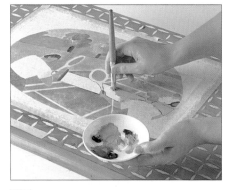

7 Tape the fourth stencil in place and stencil the racquet and racquet handle in brown, and the net in mint green. Allow to dry and remove the stencil.

8 Repeat the stenciled picture on the front panel of the box, reversing the stencils to produce a mirror image of the lid picture. Allow to dry and finish the box with a coat of clear wax.

Bathroom cabinet

Give an ordinary cupboard a jaunty nautical tone with a bold rope-and-anchor design. The motif is created with four stencils. Use our color scheme or coordinate it with the decor in your own bathroom. Before stenciling, the cupboard was given a soft colorwash treatment (see page 50) in watery tones of blue and green.

YOU WILL NEED

- ◆ **1 small cupboard**
- ◆ **Acrylic paint in blue, green, red, white and brown**
- ◆ **Clear acetate and acetate pen**
- ◆ **Anchor, lifebelt and rope templates** *(see page 147)*
- ◆ **Craft knife and cutting mat**
- ◆ **Stencil brush**
- ◆ **Masking tape**
- ◆ **Clear acrylic varnish**

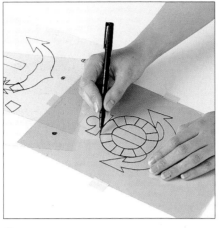

1 Colorwash the cupboard in blue and green. Allow it to dry. Using the acetate pen, trace the anchor and rope templates onto separate pieces of acetate.

2 Using the craft knife and cutting mat, carefully cut out the anchor, two lifebelt and rope stencils, giving four separate stencils in all.

3 Tape the anchor stencil in position on the door. Using the stencil brush, fill in with blue acrylic. Allow to dry. Remove stencil.

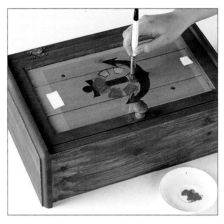

4 Tape the first lifebelt stencil in position over the anchor. Stencil with red acrylic. Allow it to dry. Remove the stencil.

5 Tape the second lifebelt stencil in position over the first. Stencil with white acrylic. Allow it to dry. Remove the stencil.

6 Tape the rope stencil in position. Stencil with brown acrylic, adding highlights in white. Remove stencil. Finish with three coats of varnish.

Card case

Perhaps it holds only the lunchtime sandwiches, but this rectangular box doubles as an attaché case which happens to be just the right size for carrying the accoutrements of the accomplished gambler. The witty trompe l'oeil *motif transforms an ordinary object into something absolutely ace!*

YOU WILL NEED

- ◆ 1 wooden attaché case
- ◆ Green latex paint
- ◆ Card and dice stencils *(see page 150)*
- ◆ Clear acetate and acetate pen
- ◆ Craft knife and cutting mat
- ◆ Chalk or pencil
- ◆ Masking tape
- ◆ Acrylic paint in white, black, red, pale gray and dark gray
- ◆ Stencil brush
- ◆ Fine artist's brush
- ◆ Clear acrylic varnish

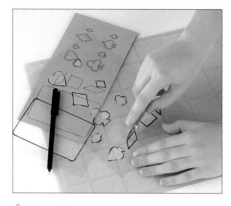

1 Paint the case green. Scale up the stencils, trace them onto acetate and cut out, using a craft knife and cutting mat. You will have 20 stencils.

2 Mark on the case the positions for the cards and border. Tape the card stencil in place. Using white acrylic, stencil the card along the left-hand edge first, then graduate the color from left to right. Allow to dry and remove the stencil.

3 Stencil on the suit as required in appropriate colors. Stencil on three more cards in a similar way, fanning them out to the right, overlapping them and stenciling on the suits as you go.

4 Using white acrylic, stencil on the dice shape at various angles in corners and centers of each side. Stencil the white outlines of the suits as shown first, then the inner shapes in appropriate colors on top.

5 Using two shades of gray, stencil on the dice sides. Using a fine brush, hand-paint the dots in black. Allow to dry and finish with three coats of clear acrylic varnish.

Chess table

*Employ some elegant gamesmanship with a stenciled chess table that
will fold away into an odd corner when the game is over. The stencil is a scroll
repeated in simpler form on the legs and edges with subtle highlights in gold and silver.
The board can be executed in several ways. The easiest is to photocopy the illustration
on page 151. Alternatively, cut individual squares from marbled paper
and stick them down, carefully butting the edges together.*

YOU WILL NEED

- 1 small oblong folding table
- Black and cream latex paint
- Masking tape
- Scroll stencils *(see page 150)*
- Clear acetate and acetate pen
- Craft knife and cutting mat
- Acrylic paint in white, black, gold and silver
- Stencil brush
- Fine artist's brush
- Chessboard *(see page 151)*
- White craft glue
- Clear acrylic varnish
- Acrylic varnish in "antique pine"

The right move

When you are glueing down the chessboard or the marbled paper squares on the table-top panel, make sure that you position the squares correctly. As the players look at the board, a black square should be in the top right-hand corner.

1 Paint the table top cream and the rest black. Mark a square central chessboard panel on the top and a rectangular one for the scroll stencil on each side of the square. Mask with tape and paint scroll panels black.

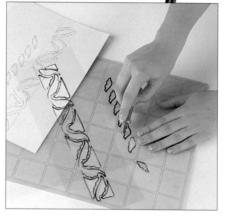

2 Scale up the scroll stencil to fit the side panels, and the border stencil to fit the table edge and legs. Trace the stencils onto acetate. Cut them out using a craft knife and cutting mat.

3 Tape the scroll stencil in position on the side panel. Stipple lightly with white acrylic, then stipple over the white with gold highlights. Allow to dry. Repeat on other side panel and the cross-strut between the legs.

4 Beginning at a corner, tape the border stencil to the top edge. Fill in with black acrylic, adding silver highlights and moving the stencil around the edge as the paint dries.

5 Stencil border on the outside of the legs with white, adding gold highlights. Using a fine brush, paint a gold rule on the side edges. Paint the square panel on the top black.

6 Photocopy the chessboard on page 151, enlarging it to fit the panel. Cut out and glue down. Allow to dry. Finish with four coats of clear and one coat of colored varnish.

Paper cut-outs

*P*aper cutting is a very direct, simple craft, making use of readily available materials that would often have been discarded. It is traditionally associated with folk or peasant traditions in countries such as Mexico where brightly colored cut-outs are used on ceremonial occasions. In India, too, three-dimensional paper stars made by folding and cutting are hung up to celebrate Diwali. In Poland, folk decoration makes use of stylized flower and animal cut-outs. The Chinese are well-known for their inventiveness with paper in all its forms – their approach is wonderfully bold and colorful – and the charming English 19th-century vogue for silhouette portraits required a high degree of skill in the art of paper-cutting. In fact, paper cut-outs may be the one craft that almost everybody has indulged in at some time. Children will be familiar with folding and cutting a paper strip to produce dancing ladies, and most of us will have cut out paper stars, snowflakes and trees to decorate Christmas cards.

Paper cut-outs can be used to create complete landscapes, abstract patterns, elegant borders or witty figurative motifs. Since you can work at any scale, anything from greetings cards to complete walls can be decorated. Chests of drawers, cupboards, doors and even the edges of floors can be enhanced with paper cut-outs. On small objects such as frames and boxes more delicate cutting can be employed.

Materials

Paper You can make good use of the range of papers available for cut-outs – from the thinnest of colored tissue to heavier marbled and mottled textures. Depending on the required effect, medium-weight or lighter papers are most suitable and will produce the smoothest finish. Papers with inlaid textures can be effective but avoid those with too much surface texture. Some papers will shed color when glued or varnished, so seal them before using with diluted white craft glue as for découpage. It is also advisable to seal printed papers before sticking them down.

Adhesive Most medium-weight papers can be stuck down with white craft glue. Use a gluestick for anything more delicate as it is less likely to stretch the paper.

Paint Mat latex paint provides a good smooth background surface for paper cut-outs.

Varnish All paper cut-out work will need to be sealed and protected by several coats of clear varnish. The principles of applying it are the same as for découpage (see page 23). Acrylic varnish is suitable unless oil-based products have been used in the base coat, in which case use polyurethane.

Equipment

Scissors Cutting tools are the most important pieces of equipment for paper cut-outs. You will need at least two good pairs of scissors – one medium-sized, straight-bladed pair for the bulk of the work and one pair of manicure scissors with curved blades for more intricate cutting.

Craft knife and cutting mat These can be useful for delicate cutting and for making small "interior" cuts in a design. You will need plenty of replacement blades as they tend to blunt quickly with such heavy use.

Rulers Use a metal ruler with a craft knife and cutting mat to cut straight lines. Any ruler can be used to help tear straight lines.

Brushes Household paint brushes are needed for applying base coats and for varnishing. Fine artist's brushes can be useful for applying adhesive to small cut-outs.

CHECKLIST
- Papers in a variety of colors and textures
- White craft glue
- Gluestick
- Latex paint
- Clear varnish
- Medium-sized scissors
- Curved manicure scissors
- Craft knife
- Cutting mat
- Rulers
- Household paint brushes
- Artist's brushes

Paper cut-outs techniques

Some of the techniques are identical to those of découpage (see pages 22–23). But there are also some cunning cutting, tearing and folding techniques which provide enormous potential for original and exciting cut-out effects.

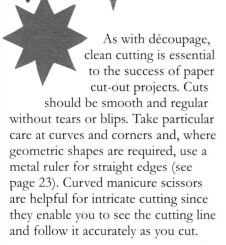

CUTTING PAPER

As with découpage, clean cutting is essential to the success of paper cut-out projects. Cuts should be smooth and regular without tears or blips. Take particular care at curves and corners and, where geometric shapes are required, use a metal ruler for straight edges (see page 23). Curved manicure scissors are helpful for intricate cutting since they enable you to see the cutting line and follow it accurately as you cut.

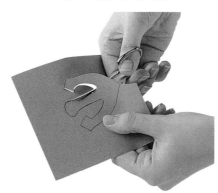

Using curved scissors Hold the scissors with the thumb and middle finger of your cutting hand with the curves pointing away from you. Begin at the lower edge of the shape to be cut and feed the paper into the blades rather than moving the scissors.

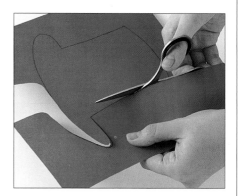

Cutting into corners Using straight-bladed scissors, cut from the outside down one side of the corner carefully into the point and stop. Remove the scissors from the paper, then cut from the other side into the point. Do not turn the scissors at the point.

TEARING PAPER

Tearing rather than cutting the edges of paper shapes provides another freer dimension to paper collage. Some papers – tissue paper and rough-textured papers, for example – lend themselves especially well to this technique. It is also particularly suitable for areas of a design – vegetation, water, clouds – which naturally have an indeterminate rather than a hard edge. The Landscape Tray on page 108 shows how the contrast of cut and torn shapes can be very effective. You can tear the shapes in a random way or use penciled guidelines. When tearing straight lines, tear against a ruler. Some papers have a "grain" like fabric and this can affect the ease with which it tears. Make sure you are tearing along the grain not against it.

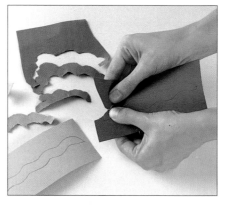

Using guidelines for tearing Pencil a rough outline of the shape required on the wrong side of the paper, either of a single sheet, or a wad of sheets for several similar shapes. Press your thumbnail into the guideline as you tear with the other fingers. For greater control, make a series of small tears, rather than long ones.

Using a ruler Tear one sheet at a time and pencil in guidelines on the wrong side of the paper if necessary. Place a ruler on top of the sheet close against the guideline. Hold it firmly down with one end across the edge of the paper. Lift the edge of the paper and tear it swiftly back against the ruler.

FOLDING AND CUTTING

Folding paper in various ways before cutting makes it possible to produce highly intricate symmetrical designs. In essence this is simply a development of the well-known children's game of "dancing ladies." The paper can be folded one or more times depending on the shape and level of detail required. It can be folded one way and cut, then opened out and folded another way and cut. By always cutting into folds, you avoid the problem of cutting tiny interior shapes in a design. The finest folded and cut work can be almost as light and delicate as lace.

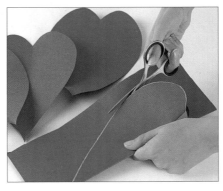

Single folds This is an easy way to cut a symmetrical shape around one axis – a heart or triangle for example. Fold the paper loosely in half (do not press the fold to a sharp crease). Draw half the motif along the fold and cut out.

Folding and cutting a square Cut out a square or a circle and fold it in half twice along the straight edges, then once along the diagonal. Trim the cut edges and make cuts in the folds, then open out.

Refold the square along the straight edges twice more if required, then along the diagonal across the corners. Make more cuts in the folds. Open out and refold again as many times as required.

Folding and cutting a circle Cut out a circle and fold in half twice. Draw the motif on the quadrant, making sure it crosses the folds on both sides to hold the circle together.

Cut out the motif carefully and open it out. Any creases will be smoothed out when the motif is stuck down on the surface.

BORDERS

Repeat-pattern borders can be made by folding a strip of paper concertina fashion and cutting out either motifs or abstract patterns.

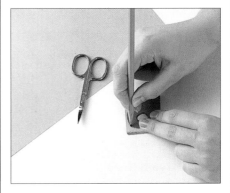

Cut a strip of paper the required depth and length of the border. Fold it concertina fashion the width of the motif or pattern repeat. If necessary, draw the motif onto the paper, making sure it crosses the folds on both sides. Alternatively, make the cuts freehand.

Cut out the motif carefully through all the layers of folded paper, making sure you do not cut off the folds. Open out the border and stick it down.

Landscape tray

Brighten up breakfasts in bed or afternoon teas
in the garden with this picturesque wooden tray.
Torn and cut paper shapes are pieced together
to make a lovely landscape. Several coats of clear
acrylic varnish over the picture will make a
practical durable finish.

YOU WILL NEED

- ◆ **1 plain wooden tray**
- ◆ **Sky blue latex paint**
- ◆ **Chalk**
- ◆ **Variety of colored papers**
- ◆ **White craft glue**
- ◆ **Clear acrylic varnish**
- ◆ **Colored acrylic varnish in "antique pine"**

Cutting and tearing

Your landscape picture can be a favorite scene from a real village or town, or a fabulous fantasy. Use cut-outs for the regular shapes you will need for buildings and torn paper for softer shapes such as trees and bushes.

1 Paint the tray blue and allow it to dry. Using white chalk, mark out a rectangle in the middle of the tray for the boundary of the landscape.

2 Using suitable colors, tear paper shapes for the background. Make use of the straight edges of the paper for the outside edge of the picture.

3 Cut out paper shapes for houses, plus details such as roofs, doors and windows. Make them up into complete buildings and glue together.

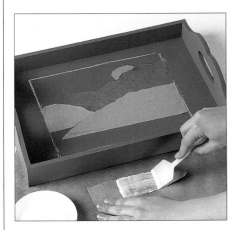

4 Arrange the background shapes in position, beginning with the shapes furthest away and overlapping them as shown. Glue them down.

5 Position houses and glue down. Allow to dry. Remove chalk marks. Apply six coats of clear acrylic varnish.

6 Apply a coat of colored varnish and, while it is still wet, wipe off the excess with a cloth. Allow to dry.

Top-hat box

Top a hat box with a dashing motif made up of layers of paper shapes. Paper cut-out designs are endlessly flexible. For example, the top hats could be sized down and arranged around the sides. The dark reds and black give the box an "around midnight" feel which will look just dandy in any budding Fred Astaire's bedroom.

YOU WILL NEED
- 1 large card hat box
- Latex paint in cream, red, blue and black

- Pair of compasses
- Top-hat and cane templates
  (see page 152)

- Colored papers in black, red, white and blue
- Clear acrylic varnish

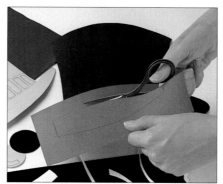

1 Paint the box cream inside and out. Allow to dry. Paint the lid sides black. Find the center, and with a pair of compasses mark a border around the lid and another just inside the first one. Paint the outer border red and the inner one blue.

2 Copy the template shapes, sizing up or down if necessary. Transfer them to colored papers: black for the top-hat shape, the hat band stripes and the cane, red for the hat band, white for the highlights. Cut out carefully.

3 Make up the hat shapes first. Stick the highlights down on the hat and on the cane shapes. Stick down the black stripes on the hat band, then the hat band on the hat.

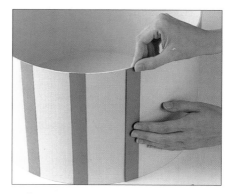

4 Glue down the hat in position on the box overlapping the border slightly as shown. Glue down the cane across the hat at an angle. Allow to dry thoroughly.

5 Measure around the box and divide it into suitable widths for stripes. Mark the stripe positions on the box sides. Cut out strips of blue paper to fit the stripes. Glue down.

6 Allow the stripes to dry and finish the box with about three coats of clear acrylic varnish. If required, attach cord and tassel fastenings as shown on page 31.

Day for night
For the appropriate setting, change from evening dress into morning dress with an alternative colorway on the top hat. Blacks, reds and whites give way to soft grays, blue and cream.

Children's boxes

*These colorful little boxes are ideal projects for children to make, and they will store
all kinds of treasures. The motif shapes can be cut out of colored papers
or ready-gummed paper which is even easier for small fingers to handle.*

DANCERS BOX

YOU WILL NEED
- 1 small round card box
- Green latex paint
- Colored paper in deep pink, pale
  pink, lilac, blue and yellow
- Dancers and animal templates
  (see page 153)
- White craft glue
- Clear acrylic varnish

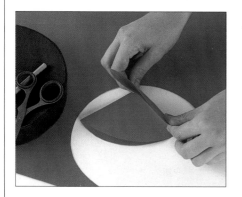

1 Paint the box green. Allow to dry.
Trace around the box lid onto deep
pink paper and cut it out. Fold the
circle of paper in half then in half
again to make a quadrant.

2 Copy the dancers template, sizing
it to fit the quadrant. Cut it out.
Trace around it onto the quadrant,
ensuring it touches the fold on both
sides. Cut out through all four layers.

3 Open out the paper circle and
glue it down on the box lid. Cut
out four bow ties and aprons in
various colors. Glue them down in
position on the dancers.

4 Copy animal templates, sizing to
fit. Transfer to folded yellow
paper. Cut two pairs each of rabbits
and birds. Glue around the box. Allow
to dry. Finish with clear varnish.

STEAMBOAT BOX

YOU WILL NEED
- **1 square box**
- **Dark blue latex paint**
- **Boat templates** *(see page 153)*
- **Colored paper in yellow (for the hull and flagpole), orange (cabin and portholes), red (stripes), pale blue (waves) and mid-blue (anchor, portholes and sea), pale and dark gray (steam), white (flag, stripe, funnel)**
- **White craft glue**
- **Clear acrylic varnish**

Folding and cutting
The dancers on one box and the waves around the sides of the other are cut from folded paper. For the dancers, the paper is folded into a quadrant, giving four motifs; for the waves, a strip for each side is concertina-folded for the number of motifs.

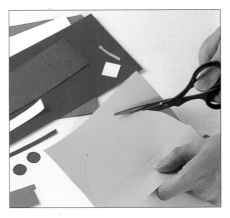

1 Paint the box blue. Allow it to dry. Copy the boat templates, sizing the design to fit the box lid. Transfer all the template shapes except the waves and the steam onto colored paper. Cut them out.

2 On pale and dark gray paper, draw rough shapes for the steam, using the template as a guide. Tear around them carefully. Similarly, draw the wave shapes for the lid on pale and mid-blue paper and carefully tear around them.

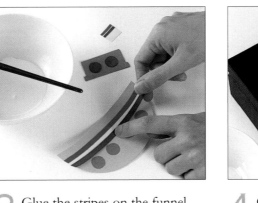

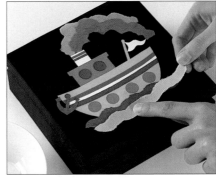

3 Glue the stripes on the funnel, and portholes on the cabin and hull. Glue red and blue stripes to the white stripe. Glue the made-up stripe to the hull.

4 Glue the hull, cabin, funnel, steam and waves on the box, overlapping the two wave shapes and the two steam shapes. Add the anchor, flag and flagpole.

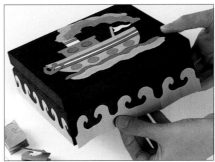

5 Cut four strips of blue paper the width of the box. Size the wave crest to fit each side an even number of times. Concertina-fold the strips to the wave crest width. Transfer the template. Cut out. Glue down. Allow to dry. Finish with clear varnish.

Shining shades

Lamplight shining through a mosaic of colored tissue makes the shades look almost like stained glass. The paper shapes are cut or torn and pieced together into a beautiful kaleidoscope of glowing color.

FLOWER SHADE

*Shapes cut from thick paper produce
a scattering of floral silhouettes against
the translucent glow of a bright
yellow background.*

YOU WILL NEED
- 1 lampshade
- White craft glue
- Flower template *(see page 153)*
- Colored thick paper in red and black
- Scrap paper
- Colored tissue paper in yellow, green and red
- Gluestick

1 Seal the shade with diluted glue. Allow to dry. Copy the template, sizing up or down if required. Transfer to colored paper and cut out five red and five black flowers.

2 Draw around the shade on scrap paper for a template. Use it to cut sheets of yellow tissue to cover the shade, and red and green strips (outer edge cut, inner edge torn) for borders.

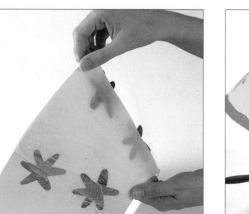

4 Working in sections, paint diluted glue over the shade and, while still wet, lay the pieces of yellow tissue over the shade to cover it completely.

3 Using a gluestick, glue the flower shapes at random over the shade, alternating red and black. Allow to dry.

5 Brush a strip of diluted glue around the top and bottom of the shade and lay down the red and green paper strips. Seal with diluted glue. Allow to dry.

LANDSCAPE SHADE

*Any ordinary plain shade can be swiftly
transformed into a beautiful sunny scene
with a collage of irregular colored shapes
made up of torn tissue paper.*

YOU WILL NEED
- 1 plain lampshade
- White craft glue
- Colored tissue paper in yellow, blue, purple, red, orange and green
- Gluestick

2 Out of yellow tissue tear an irregular circle for the sun. Tear enough pieces of blue for the sky, and purple and red for the hills.

4 Tear orange circles for the main flowers and red pieces for flower centers and petals. Stick down the red shapes on top of the orange. Stick flowers on the background.

MOSAIC SHADE

Stick small paper tissue squares all over a plain shade to create a jostling mosaic of color. Stick them down randomly or, as here, in a simple geometric pattern.

YOU WILL NEED
◆ **1 plain lampshade**
◆ **White craft glue**
◆ **Scrap paper**
◆ **Dressmaker's chalk**
◆ **Colored tissue paper in green, red, purple, blue and yellow**
◆ **Craft knife**
◆ **Gluestick**

1 Seal the shade with glue diluted one to one with water. Allow to dry. Sketch outlines of grassy shapes on folded green tissue, Tear along the lines. Make enough to circle the frame.

1 Seal the shade with glue, diluted one to one with water. Allow to dry. Cut a 1½in (4cm) square template out of scrap paper.

3 Using a gluestick, glue down the background shapes – first the sun, then sky and hills, overlapping them freely to create a background landscape.

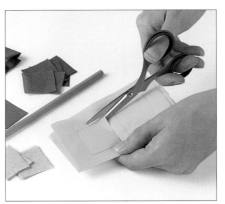

2 Fold the tissue paper several times to make a wad. Place the template on top and draw around it. Then cut out to make lots of colored tissue squares.

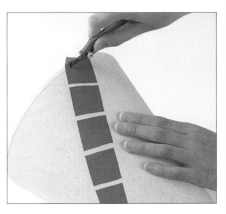

3 Using chalk, mark parallel diagonal guidelines around the shade. Stick down tissue squares along the lines, trimming off excess at top and bottom with a craft knife.

5 Finally, stick down the grassy shapes along the bottom edge of the frame to overlap the lower edges of the flowers. Seal with diluted glue. Allow to dry.

4 Continue sticking down the tissue squares, alternating rows of green tissue squares with rows of multi-colored squares. Allow to dry.

Storage bins

A brace of bins in coordinated colors are given a speedy makeover with cut-out paper shapes cleverly crafted from folded paper. Different effects can be created using smooth, handmade and inlaid papers.

HEARTS BIN

YOU WILL NEED

- 1 storage or wastepaper bin
- Blue and red latex paint
- Heart templates *(see page 152)*
- Craft knife and cutting mat
- Colored papers in red and blue
- White craft glue
- Clear acrylic varnish

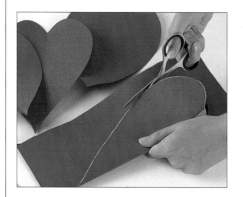

1 Paint the main part of the bin blue and the border red. Allow to dry. Copy the heart templates, sizing to fit the bin sides. Fold red paper in half. Transfer template A, matching fold. Cut it out. Repeat three times more.

2 Fold the blue paper. Transfer template B, matching fold. Cut it out. Cut out the inner shapes using a craft knife and cutting mat. Repeat three times more for the other sides of the bin.

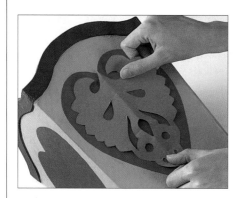

3 Unfold the red heart shapes and glue them down centrally on each side of the bin. Unfold the inner blue hearts and glue them down on top of the main shapes.

4 Using blue paper, cut out enough small hearts (C) to fit around the rim and base of the bin. Glue them down. Allow to dry. Finish with three coats of clear varnish.

FILIGREE BIN

YOU WILL NEED

- 1 storage or wastepaper bin
- Red and blue latex paint
- Colored paper in yellow, violet and mauve
  - Filigree templates *(see page 152)*
- White craft glue
- Clear acrylic varnish

1 Paint the bin red and the border blue. Allow to dry. Copy templates A, B and C, sizing them up or down if required. Cut 12 pieces of yellow paper large enough when folded once for template A. Fold each sheet in half and stack them, folds together. Transfer template A, matching folds and cut out through all layers. Unfold the paper shapes.

2 Using template B, cut out 12 shapes from violet paper in a similar way. Using template C, cut out 12 shapes from mauve paper in a similar way. Unfold all the paper shapes.

3 On each side of the bin stick down three of shapes A (the middle one upside down), three of shapes B and three of shapes C as shown. Allow to dry.

4 Using template D, cut out multi-colored triangles to fit the rim and base. Glue down. Allow to dry. Finish with clear varnish.

Papier mâché

*I*nvented in China nearly 2000 years ago, papier mâché is a traditional way of constructing three-dimensional objects using torn paper and glue. It means, literally, "mashed paper," and there are two main methods – pulping and layering. Beautiful and durable pieces are made either by sculpting and molding paper pulp, or by building up layers of paper on a base. The objects are painted, then sealed with varnish or lacquer.

Papier mâché was popular in the 19th century in Europe and the United States. Trays, platters, letter racks and boxes were made and decorated with painted flowers, birds and butterflies. In many other countries, too – notably Japan, India and Mexico – papier mâché is a well-established craft.

All the projects here use the layering technique. The base can be a china bowl or plate, or is itself constructed from thin card or corrugated cardboard before the layers of paper are applied. Using this method you can make vases, bowls, plates and picture frames in all shapes and sizes which can then be decorated in a variety of ways – hand-painting, gilding and paper collage among others.

One of the great advantages of papier mâché is that very little is needed in the way of materials or equipment. Paper, glue and paint are the basic requirements; and the paper is largely recycled, making it the most inexpensive craft of all.

Materials

Paper Good-quality newsprint works best for papier mâché. It is helpful to use different colors for alternate layers. Brightly colored newsprint makes an effective decoration. Colored papers of other kinds, such as tissue paper, can also be used for a decorative finish.

Card Corrugated cardboard and thick or thin card is often used as a base for papier mâché. Since it is to be covered, this can also be recycled material. Cardboard boxes and cereal packets are excellent sources.

Masking tape Use this for constructing card molds.

Petroleum jelly Line the china or glass bowls or plates which act as molds for the papier mâché with petroleum jelly.

Glue Use wallpaper paste for pasting layers of papier mâché. Diluted white craft glue can also be used if preferred.

Paint White latex is used to finish the surface of papier-mâché objects ready for decorating. It will preserve the characteristic rough textured surface. Use colored latex paints and acrylic paints to decorate the papier mâché.

Gesso For a smoother surface use gesso, which has a thicker and richer texture, instead of white latex as an undercoat.

Varnish Seal and protect the finished surface with clear acrylic varnish or polyurethane varnish.

Equipment

Molds The layers of papier mâché are built up on a base mold of some kind, depending on the object to be produced. It could be a bowl or plate, or the mold could itself be made of thin or thick card.

Craft knife or scalpel This is needed to trim the edges of papier-mâché bowls and plates before unmolding them. It is also useful for cutting out the shapes for card-base molds.

Sandpaper Use fine sandpaper to smooth down the rough surface of the white latex or gesso undercoat.

Brushes Ordinary household paint brushes can be used for undercoats and base coats, for applying gesso and acrylic varnish. Fine artist's brushes may be needed for surface decoration.

CHECKLIST

- ◆ **Newsprint in assorted colors**
- ◆ **Corrugated card**
- ◆ **Thin card**
- ◆ **Masking tape**
- ◆ **Petroleum jelly**
- ◆ **White craft glue**
- ◆ **Latex paint**
- ◆ **Acrylic paints**
- ◆ **Gesso**
- ◆ **Clear varnish**
- ◆ **Molds**
- ◆ **Craft knife or scalpel**
- ◆ **Fine sandpaper**
- ◆ **Paint brushes**
- ◆ **Artist's brushes**

Papier-mâché techniques

Papier mâché involves not just the decoration but the creation of an object.
Although the techniques are very simple, they can be time-consuming. Building up
layer on layer of paper and drying the bowl, frame or plate can take a week or more.

PREPARING CHINA OR GLASS MOLDS

Papier mâché is pasted down over a mold of some sort. This is often a china or glass bowl or plate. To prevent the papier mâché sticking to the mold, coat the inside (or the surface to be covered) generously with petroleum jelly. When the papier mâché is dry, gently ease it out of or off the mold by inserting a blunt knife underneath it.

PASTING THE PAPER

Mix up a large quantity of wallpaper paste following the manufacturer's instructions (it will keep well in an airtight jar or the refrigerator if it is not all used up). It is easiest to use your fingers to apply the paste to such small pieces. Paste the pieces on both sides. Drape them over the edge of the bowl until you are ready to stick them down.

COVERING THE MOLD

PREPARING THE PAPER

Tear up plenty of newsprint in advance. Tear up large pieces for large items with lots of flat area, small pieces for small, intricate or curved shapes. It is advisable to use at least two colors of newsprint, applying a different color on alternate layers. This helps to distinguish one layer from another when you are pasting them down, and so keep track of the number of layers applied.

The first layer Cover the mold with the pasted paper pieces in an even layer, taking it well beyond the sides of the mold. Make sure each piece lies flat. Smooth it gently but firmly into the shape of the mold.

The second layer Using a different color if possible, cover the mold again. The more even the layers the more regular will be the final shape. Apply at least eight layers over a bowl or plate, four over a card base.

FINISHING OFF

Allow the papier-mâché bowl or plate to dry in a warm room for at least four days. An object molded over a card base will take at least two days. It must be completely dry all through before decorating. You may need to dry it for another day to dry off the outside after removing it from the mold.

Trimming Before removing the object from the mold, trim the edge with a craft knife or scalpel. Pierce the papier mâché with the point of the knife then run it closely against the edge of the mold. Alternatively, remove the papier mâché and shape the edge as desired, following a penciled guideline if necessary.

Covering the edges Remove the papier mâché from the mold. Neaten the raw trimmed edges by covering them evenly with a layer of papier mâché. Use small strips, butt them up against each other with only the smallest overlap and smooth them down around the edge and into the sides for a regular finish.

USING A CARD BASE

A base for papier mâché can be made out of thin card or corrugated cardboard. Use thin card for as a base for curved shapes and thick corrugated card for stiff flat or flat-sided shapes.

Layers of corrugated card can also be built up into three-dimensional shapes. Use templates to mark out the shapes and cut out with scissors or a craft knife and cutting mat. Use white craft glue to stick the layers of card together. Cover with at least four layers of papier mâché, pressing it well into and around the corners.

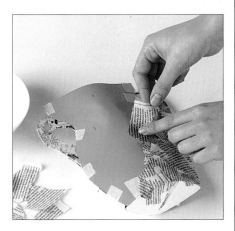

Thin card can be formed into cylindrical or other curved shapes. Hold the base together with masking tape until it is covered with papier mâché. Apply at least four layers of papier mâché, smoothing it evenly around edges and curves.

DECORATING

The papier mâché must be completely dry before it is decorated. If it is to be painted, first apply at least two coats of undiluted white latex as an undercoat. Rub the surface down lightly with fine sandpaper between coats. Apply at least two more coats of the base color.

Gesso can be used as an undercoat instead of latex. It provides a much smoother finish. Paint it on thickly in at least two coats, cross-brushing to avoid brushmarks. Sand down the surface with fine sandpaper after each coat.

Colored paper collage can also be used to decorate papier mâché. Tear colored newsprint into small pieces and apply as the final layer of papier mâché. You can also use colored tissue paper, or other light-textured papers. If the paper is translucent, apply a white latex or gesso undercoat before sticking it down.

Versatile vases

Decorate these whimsical vases with hand-painting or paper cut-out shapes. Use them as novel containers for unconventional collections — feathers, hat-pins or artificial flowers. For real blooms or plants, conceal a waterproof container inside the vase.

URN

YOU WILL NEED

- **Urn templates** *(see page 154)*
- **Thin card**
- **Masking tape**
- **Newsprint**
- **White craft glue**
- **White latex paint or gesso**
- **Pink and red latex paint**
- **Fine artist's brush**
- **Clear acrylic varnish**

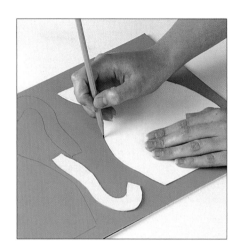

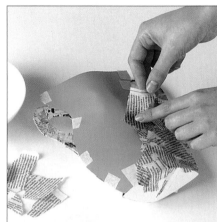

1 Copy the templates for the body, handles and base, sizing up or down if necessary. Transfer them to thin card and cut out two body shapes, four handle shapes and one base shape.

2 Tape the urn shapes together, fitting the base between the body shapes. Stick handles together in pairs and tape to the vase. Stuff the body lightly with newspaper. Cover with about three layers of papier mâché.

3 Allow to dry thoroughly for at least two days. Cover the vase with two coats of white latex (or gesso for a smooth finish). Allow to dry.

4 Paint the sides of the urn pink and the handles red. Allow it all to dry thoroughly. Using a fine artist's brush, paint parallel wavy red lines on both sides. Allow to dry. Finish with clear varnish.

HEXAGONAL VASE

YOU WILL NEED
- ◆ **Vase templates** *(see page 155)*
- ◆ **Corrugated or thick card**
- ◆ **Craft knife and cutting mat**
- ◆ **Masking tape**
- ◆ **Newsprint (two colors)**
- ◆ **Wallpaper paste**
- ◆ **White latex paint or gesso**
- ◆ **Deep and pale blue acrylic paint**
- ◆ **Colored papers to match the paint**
- ◆ **Clear satin varnish**

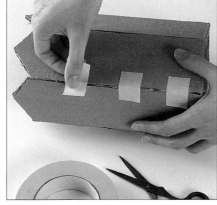

1 Copy the templates, sizing up or down if necessary. Cut them out. Trace around B (for the base) onto corrugated card and A (for the sides), repeating A side by side six times in all. Cut out using a craft knife and cutting mat.

2 Using a craft knife, score the sides of the vase along the edges of each panel. Fold the sides in along the scored lines to make a hexagonal cylinder. Using small pieces of masking tape, join the edges neatly together.

Changing shapes
Using corrugated card, you can produce different shapes. Cut a straight-sided polygon, such as a triangle or square, for the base. Size template A to equal the side measurement. Repeat it across three times for a triangle, four for a square.

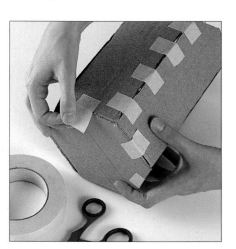

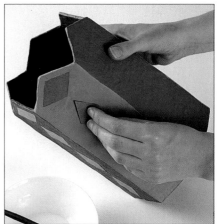

3 Fit the base shape B into position on the bottom of the vase. Using masking tape, fix it to the sides of the vase.

4 Cover the sides and base evenly with about three layers of papier mâché. Allow to dry. Paint all over inside and out with two coats of white latex (or gesso for a smoother finish).

5 Paint alternate panels deep and pale blue. Allow to dry. Cut out diamond shapes from two tones of blue paper. Glue down on the sides light on dark and dark on light. Allow to dry. Finish with clear varnish.

Bright bowls

Paint a clutch of papier-mâché bowls in bright glowing colors and decorate with sizzling stripes or simple stenciled motifs such as spirals and stars.

SPIRALS BOWL

Stencil a golden yellow bowl with a colorful tangle of whirling spirals.

YOU WILL NEED
- 1 large glass or china bowl
- Petroleum jelly
- Newsprint (two colors if possible)
- Wallpaper paste
- Craft knife and cutting mat
- White latex or gesso
- Yellow latex
- Spiral stencil *(see page 154)*
- Clear acetate and acetate pen
- Stencil brush
- Acrylic paint in red, green and purple
- Masking tape
- Clear satin acrylic varnish

1 Cover the inside of the bowl with petroleum jelly. Tear newsprint into medium pieces. Paste them with wallpaper paste using your fingers. Cover the bowl evenly with at least eight layers. Allow to dry for 2–4 days.

2 Using a craft knife trim the paper edges neatly. Remove the paper bowl from the mold and paste two layers of paper strips around the edge to neaten it. Allow to dry.

3 Paint the bowl inside and out with two coats of white latex (or gesso for a smoother finish). Allow to dry.

4 Paint the bowl with yellow latex. Allow to dry. Trace the spiral stencil onto clear acetate and cut it out using a craft knife and cutting mat.

5 Using tape to hold the stencil in position, stencil red, green and purple spirals onto the bowl inside and outside. Allow to dry and varnish with clear satin varnish.

ZIGZAG BOWL

You can trim the edge of papier-mâché bowls into attractive shapes. Wavy or zigzag edges are particularly effective. Cut the edge freehand or follow the rim of the base bowl.

YOU WILL NEED
- 1 large glass or china bowl (with zigzag edge if possible)
- Petroleum jelly
- Newsprint (two colors if possible)
- Wallpaper paste
- Craft knife
- White latex or gesso
- Orange, yellow and blue latex
- Clear satin acrylic varnish

2 Taking the paper well above the edges of the bowl, build up at least eight layers in a similar way. Allow to dry for two to four days.

4 Paste two layers of paper neatly over the edge and allow to dry. Paint the bowl with two coats of white latex (or gesso for a smoother finish). Allow to dry.

PATCHWORK BOWL

Colored newsprint torn into a crazy patchwork of shapes makes an easy instant finish for a papier-mâché bowl.

YOU WILL NEED

- ◆ 1 small glass or china bowl
- ◆ Newsprint (in two colors for the papier mâché and a variety of bright colors to decorate)
- ◆ Wallpaper paste
- ◆ Craft knife
- ◆ Base template *(see page 154)*
- ◆ Masking tape
- ◆ White craft glue
- ◆ Clear satin acrylic varnish

1 Cover the inside of the bowl with petroleum jelly. Tear up newsprint. Using your fingers, paste with wallpaper paste and cover the bowl in an even layer.

3 Trim the papier mâché with a craft knife following the zigzag rim. Or mark a zigzag line around the edge and cut it out. Remove the papier mâché from the bowl.

5 Mark out zigzag stripes to follow the edge of the bowl. Paint them orange, yellow and blue. Paint the rest of the bowl blue. Allow to dry. Finish with clear satin varnish.

1 Cover the bowl with papier mâché as given for the spirals bowl. When dry, trim the edge with a craft knife and neaten it with two layers of papier mâché.

3 Cover with three layers of papier mâché. Allow to dry. Join the base to the bowl inside and out with tape. Cover the joins with three layers of papier mâché. Allow to dry.

2 Copy the base template, sizing it up or down if necessary. Transfer to thin card and cut out. Tape the straight edges together to form a hollow cone.

4 Tear colored newsprint into irregular shapes. Paste down all over the bowl and base. Allow to dry. Seal with diluted glue. Allow to dry. Finish with satin varnish.

Paper platters

Papier-mâché plates pretty enough to hang on the wall or display on a dresser are painted in bright colors and decorated with découpage and paper cut-outs. The square plate is made from corrugated card and the oval one is molded on a plain china serving dish.

SQUARE PLATE

YOU WILL NEED
- **Plate templates** *(see page 155)*
- **Corrugated card or polyboard**
- **Craft knife and cutting mat**
- **White craft glue**
- **Newsprint (in two colors if possible)**
- **White latex or gesso**
- **Pale pink and deep pink latex paint**
- **Clean lint-free cloth**
- **Rosette templates** *(see page 155)*
- **Colored paper in pale blue and deep blue**
- **Clear satin acrylic varnish**

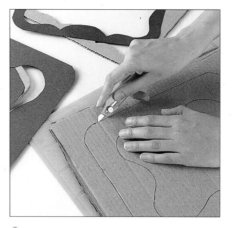

1 Copy the three templates, sizing them up or down if necessary, and cut them out. Trace around the shapes onto corrugated card and cut them out carefully using a craft knife and cutting mat.

2 Position shape B on top of shape A as shown on the template and glue them down using white craft glue. Position shape C on top of shape B and glue down. Allow to dry.

3 Tear newsprint into small pieces. Using wallpaper paste, stick the paper down on the plate in an even layer pressing well into the corners. Build up three layers, using a different color on alternate layers.

4 Allow the plate to dry for at least two days. Paint it with white latex or gesso. Allow to dry. Paint it pale pink. Allow to dry. Paint the border deep pink. Distress the paint while still wet by rubbing with a cloth.

5 Trace rosette templates onto pale and deep blue papers. Cut them out. Glue the small rosette on top of the larger one. Allow to dry. Glue them down in the middle of the plate. Finish with clear varnish.

OVAL PLATE

YOU WILL NEED

- 1 large glass or china oval plate
- Petroleum jelly
- Newsprint (two colors if possible)
- Wallpaper paste
- Craft knife
- White latex or gesso
- Latex in blue, deep blue and pink
- Fine artist's brush
- Flower motifs
- Clear satin acrylic varnish

Antique paint finishes
The plates are painted with bright pastel latex paints in two tones. The darker color is painted on, then some is rubbed off while still wet to soften the color like old faded china.

1 Cover the top plate with petroleum jelly. Tear up newsprint. Using wallpaper paste, cover the plate evenly, taking the paper beyond the edge. Build up eight layers. Allow to dry for at least two days.

2 Using a craft knife, trim neatly following the edge of the plate. Remove the papier mâché. Paste two layers of paper strips over the edge. Allow to dry. Paint with white emulsion or gesso. Allow to dry.

3 Paint the plate blue, then with darker blue paint the rim. While still wet rub with a cloth to distress it. Allow to dry. Cut out small flowers and glue down around the plate. Allow to dry.

4 Using a fine artist's brush, paint a narrow border of pink latex around the plate. Allow to dry and finish with clear satin acrylic varnish.

Fantastical frames

*These fabulous frames are made from simple card shapes covered in layers
of papier mâché. The idea can be adapted to almost any shape — ovals, circles,
diamonds, triangles or even irregular shapes. Build flat shapes into three dimensions
by adding one or more layers of card on top of the basic frame.*

GOLD SCROLL FRAME

YOU WILL NEED
- **Gold scroll frame templates** *(see page 156)*
- **Corrugated card or polyboard**
- **Craft knife and cutting mat**
- **White craft glue**
- **Newsprint (two colors if possible)**
- **Wallpaper paste**
- **White latex or gesso**
- **Yellow ocher latex paint**
- **Brown and gold acrylic paint**
- **Clear satin acrylic varnish**

1 Copy the templates, sizing them up or down if necessary. Transfer them onto card as follows: one main frame A and four each of side pieces B and C. Cut them out.

2 Position the side pieces B on top of main frame A as shown on the template. Glue them down using white craft glue. Allow to dry.

3 Position the side pieces C on top of B as shown in the template. Glue them down using white craft glue. Allow to dry.

4 Tear newsprint into strips. Using wallpaper paste, stick them down on the frame in an even layer, pressing well into the corners. Build up about three layers. Allow to dry for at least two days.

5 Paint the frame all over with gesso or white latex. Allow to dry. Paint with yellow latex. Allow to dry. Paint layer B brown and layer C with gold acrylic. Allow to dry. Finish with clear satin acrylic varnish.

GREEN DECO FRAME

YOU WILL NEED

- **Green deco frame template**
  (see page 157)
- **Corrugated card or polyboard**
- **Craft knife and cutting mat**
- **White craft glue**
- **Newsprint (two colors if possible)**
- **Wallpaper paste**
- **White latex or gesso**
- **Green latex paint**
- **Pale green and copper acrylic paint**
- **Clear satin acrylic varnish**

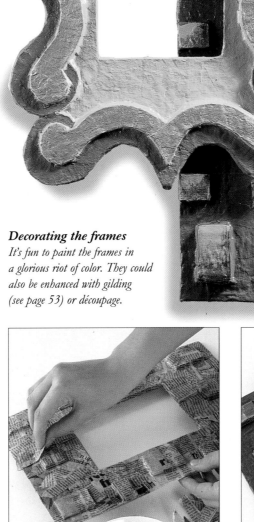

Decorating the frames
It's fun to paint the frames in a glorious riot of color. They could also be enhanced with gilding (see page 53) or découpage.

1 Copy the template, sizing it up or down if necessary. Transfer it onto card. Cut it out using a craft knife and cutting mat. Cut small rectangles from another strip of card.

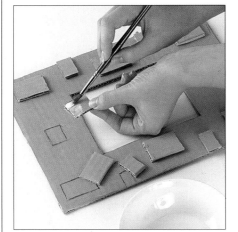

2 Position the small rectangles on top of the main frame as shown on the template. Glue them down using white craft glue. Allow to dry.

3 Tear newsprint into strips. Using wallpaper paste, stick them down on the frame in an even layer, pressing well into the corners. Build up about three layers. Allow to dry for at least two days.

4 Paint the frame all over with gesso. Allow to dry. Paint it green. Paint the rectangles pale green. Allow to dry. Lightly brush copper acrylic onto the rectangles. Allow to dry. Finish with clear satin varnish.

Templates, stencils and motifs

Photocopy the images and designs, enlarging or reducing them as required (see page 18). Hand-tint découpage images if necessary (see page 22). Trace stencils directly onto clear acetate or transfer them to stencil paper using carbon paper (see page 74). Templates for paper cut-out shapes can be transferred in a similar way.

Stars and cupids (p30)
The hat box is découpaged with a variety of cupids and stars. Photocopy the cupids and use any of the star templates to cut out stars from silver paper.

Scroll box (p36)

These three scroll motifs are pieced together
on the scroll box. Sizing up or down if necessary,
copy the pair of scrolls (shown twice here)
three times and the centerpiece five times.

Piazza boxes (p37)

Copy the piazza motif enough times
to fit around the box, sizing it
up or down if necessary.

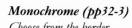

Monochrome (pp32-3)

Choose from the border designs (left and below) and copy them as required, sizing up or down if necessary to fit the containers, shelf unit and peg rack.

Music box (pp26-7)

Make nine copies of the dancer motif: one sized to fit the box lid and eight sized to fit the sides.

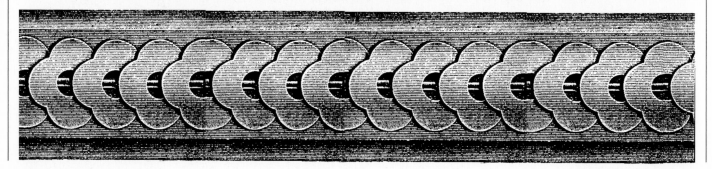

Fruit bowl (p40)
Copy the template, sizing it up or down if necessary. Transfer to colored paper and cut one outline shape and three separate heart shapes.

Cat and bow (p31)
Copy the bow stencil, sizing it up or down if necessary. Trace it onto clear acetate.

Vase of flowers (p40)
Copy the vase template, sizing it up or down if necessary. Transfer to colored paper. Cut out one outline shape.

Wild strawberries (p42)
Copy the heart shape, sizing it up to fit the cupboard door. Cut out and trace around it onto the door.

B O R D E R

Celtic box (p55)

Sizing them up or down if necessary, copy the border stencil and stencils A (following the solid line) and B (following the dashed line). Trace separately onto clear acetate.

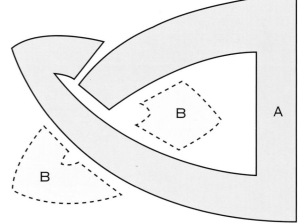

Gift wrap (pp56-7)

Copy the leaf stencils, sizing up or down if necessary. Trace them onto clear acetate for positive stencils and onto stiff paper or stencil paper for negative stencils.

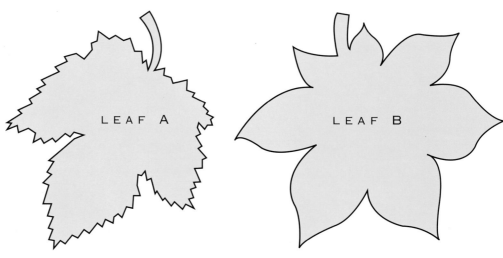

L E A F   A

L E A F   B

Ageing gracefully (pp58-9)

Sizing up or down if necessary, copy the flower or leaf template. Transfer the flower to a potato printing block and cut around. Transfer the leaf to a sponge printing block and cut it out.

F L O W E R

L E A F

FRONT
SCROLL

BACK
SCROLL

BACK
SCROLL

Stationery set (pp76-7)
*Copy the three scroll stencils, sizing
up or down if necessary. Trace them
onto clear acetate templates for the
back and front of the letter rack.*

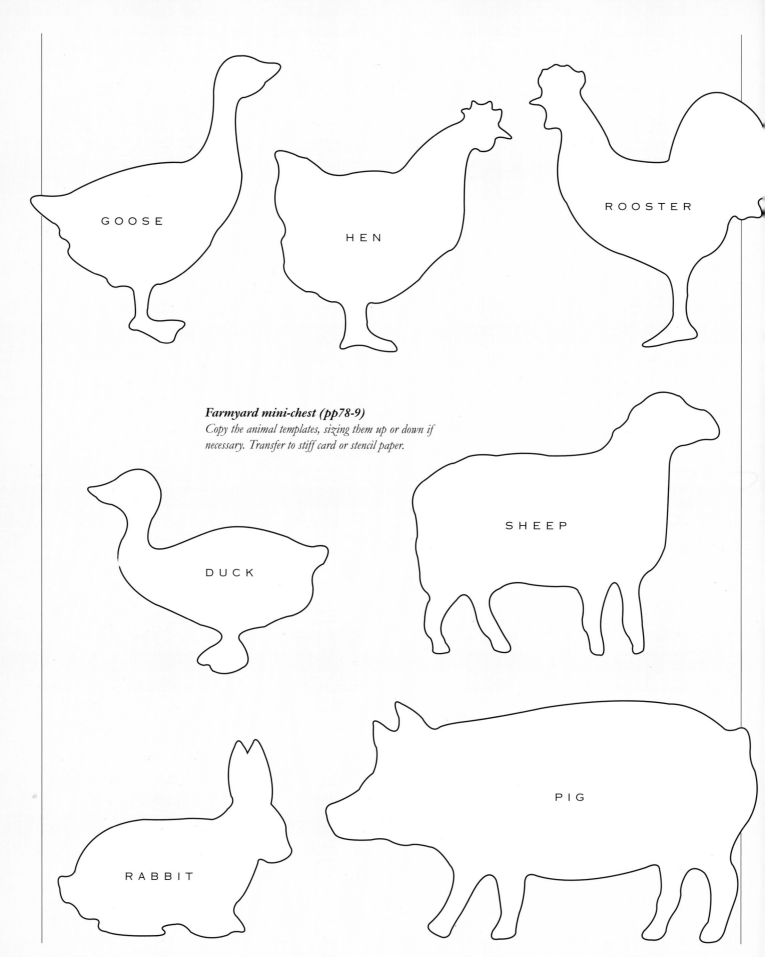

GOOSE

HEN

ROOSTER

Farmyard mini-chest (pp78-9)
Copy the animal templates, sizing them up or down if
necessary. Transfer to stiff card or stencil paper.

DUCK

SHEEP

RABBIT

PIG

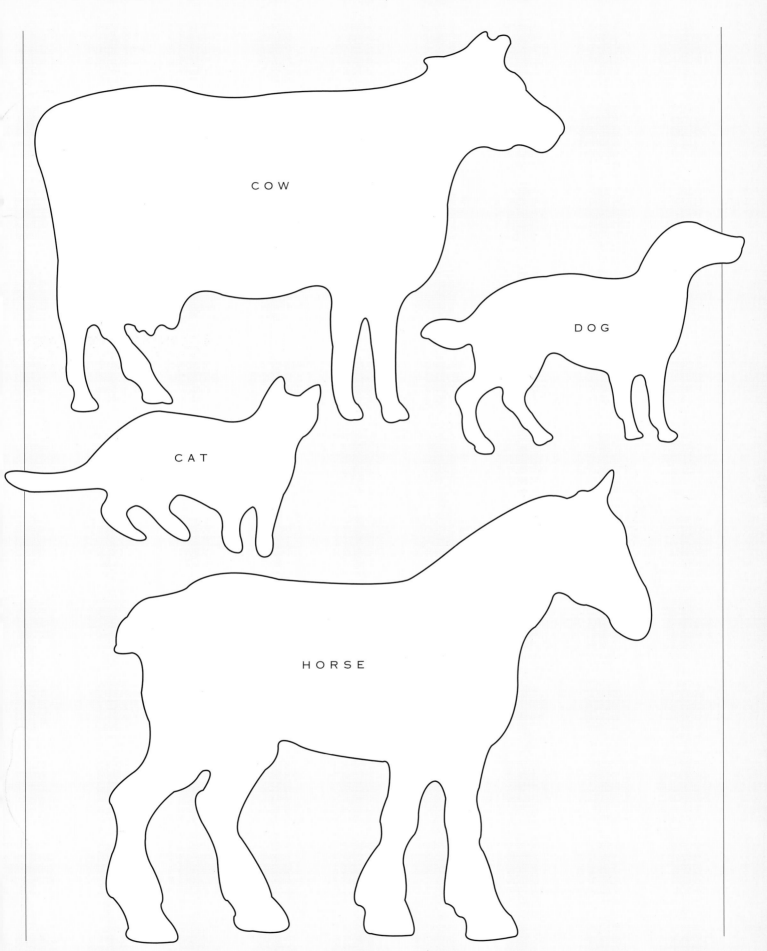

COW

DOG

CAT

HORSE

Fruity bucket (p82)
There are two stencils for this
design: A (left) and B (below).
Copy the stencils, sizing up or
down if necessary, and transfer to
stencil paper.

FRUIT B

FRUIT A

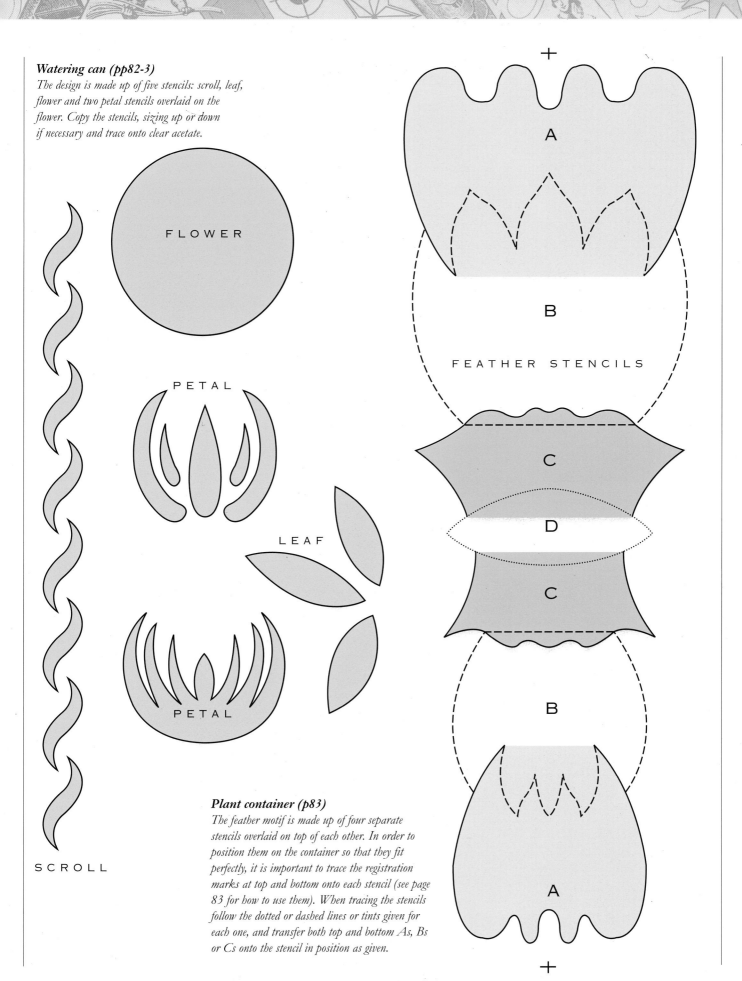

Watering can (pp82-3)

The design is made up of five stencils: scroll, leaf, flower and two petal stencils overlaid on the flower. Copy the stencils, sizing up or down if necessary and trace onto clear acetate.

FLOWER

PETAL

LEAF

PETAL

SCROLL

A

B

FEATHER STENCILS

C

D

C

B

A

Plant container (p83)

The feather motif is made up of four separate stencils overlaid on top of each other. In order to position them on the container so that they fit perfectly, it is important to trace the registration marks at top and bottom onto each stencil (see page 83 for how to use them). When tracing the stencils follow the dotted or dashed lines or tints given for each one, and transfer both top and bottom As, Bs or Cs onto the stencil in position as given.

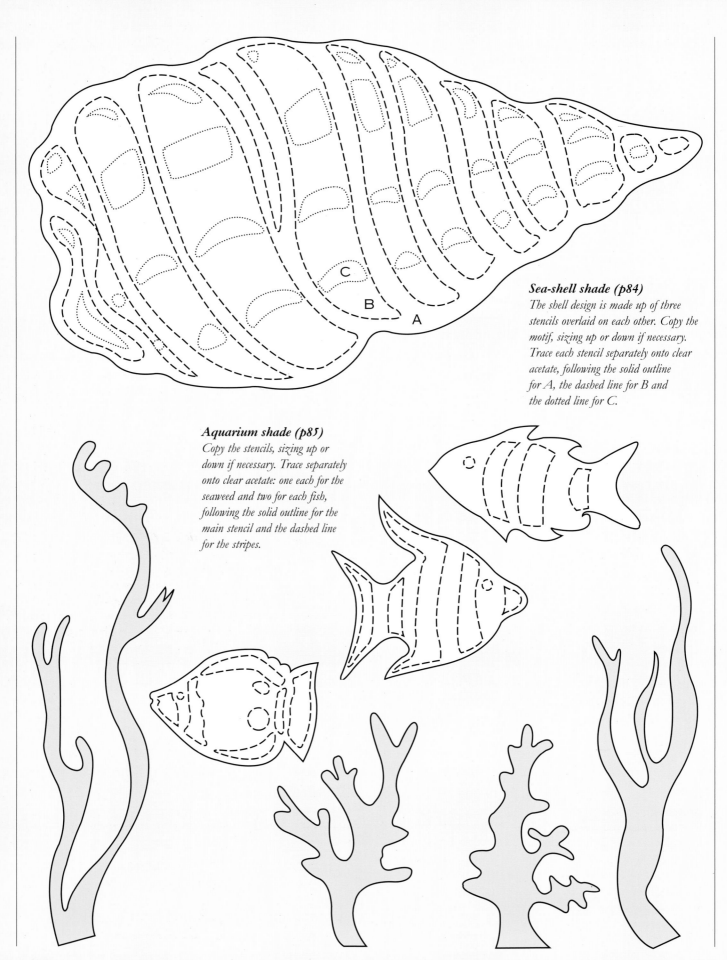

Sea-shell shade (p84)

The shell design is made up of three stencils overlaid on each other. Copy the motif, sizing up or down if necessary. Trace each stencil separately onto clear acetate, following the solid outline for A, the dashed line for B and the dotted line for C.

Aquarium shade (p85)

Copy the stencils, sizing up or down if necessary. Trace separately onto clear acetate: one each for the seaweed and two for each fish, following the solid outline for the main stencil and the dashed line for the stripes.

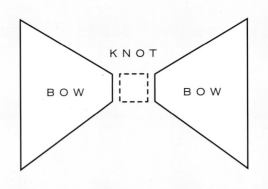

Bow-tie geometrics (p91)
*Copy the bow, knot and border
stencils, sizing up or down if
necessary. Trace separately onto
clear acetate.*

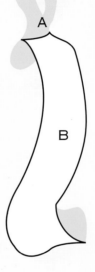

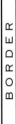

Tartan tie box (p90)
*Copy the template, sizing up or
down if necessary. Cut it out and
use as a position guide for masking
tape stencils as shown on page 90.*

Banner tray (p86)
*Copy the double banner design,
sizing it up to fit the tray.
Following the shaded areas for
stencil A and the unshaded areas
for stencil B, trace onto separate
clear acetate templates. Remember
to trace both banners in position
onto each template.*

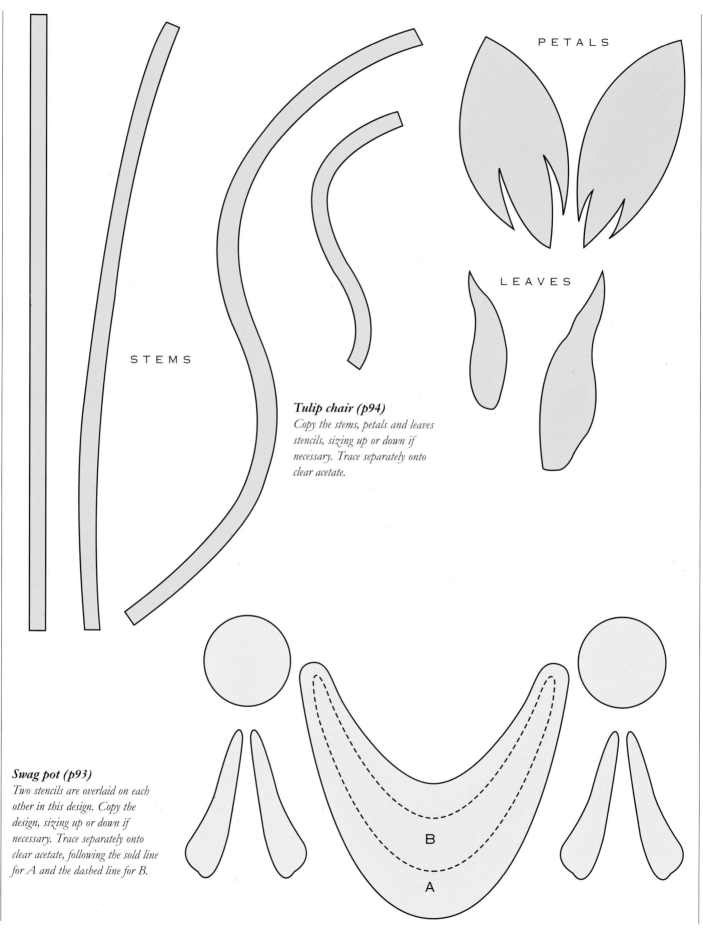

PETALS

STEMS

LEAVES

Tulip chair (p94)
Copy the stems, petals and leaves stencils, sizing up or down if necessary. Trace separately onto clear acetate.

Swag pot (p93)
Two stencils are overlaid on each other in this design. Copy the design, sizing up or down if necessary. Trace separately onto clear acetate, following the sold line for A and the dashed line for B.

B

A

Trailing ivy trough (p92)
Copy the stencil, sizing it up or
down if necessary. Trace onto clear
acetate. Cut out the leaves only –
the stems and tendrils are
guidelines for hand-painting.

**Bathroom cabinet
(pp98-9)**
The anchor design is made
up of four stencils: the rope,
the anchor and two lifebelt
stencils (one for each color).
Copy the design, sizing it
up or down if necessary, and
trace the stencils separately
onto clear acetate. Add
registration marks if
required to position the
stencils accurately.

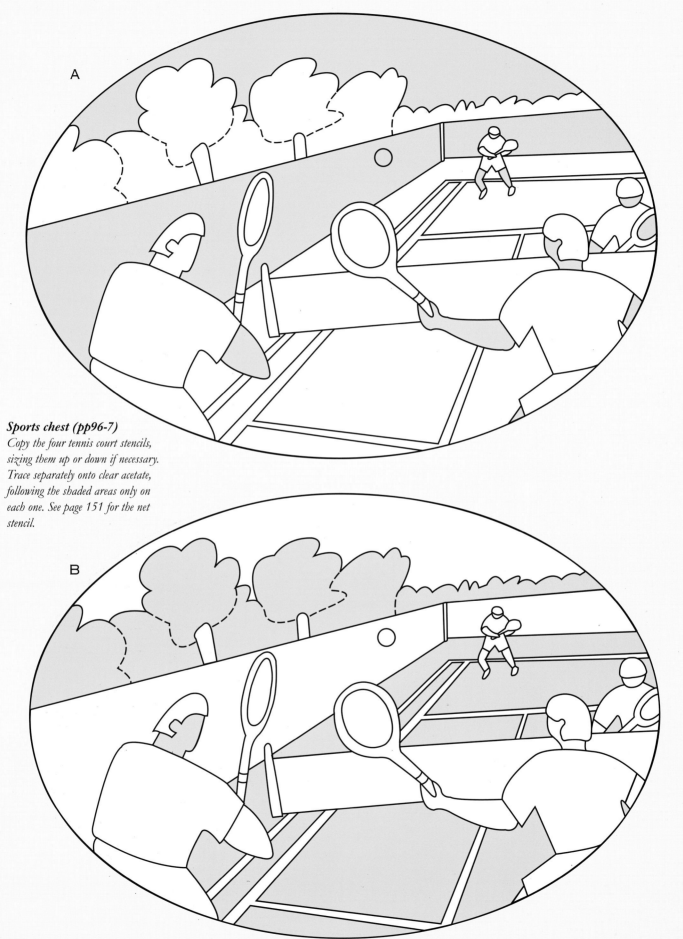

A

Sports chest (pp96-7)
*Copy the four tennis court stencils,
sizing them up or down if necessary.
Trace separately onto clear acetate,
following the shaded areas only on
each one. See page 151 for the net
stencil.*

B

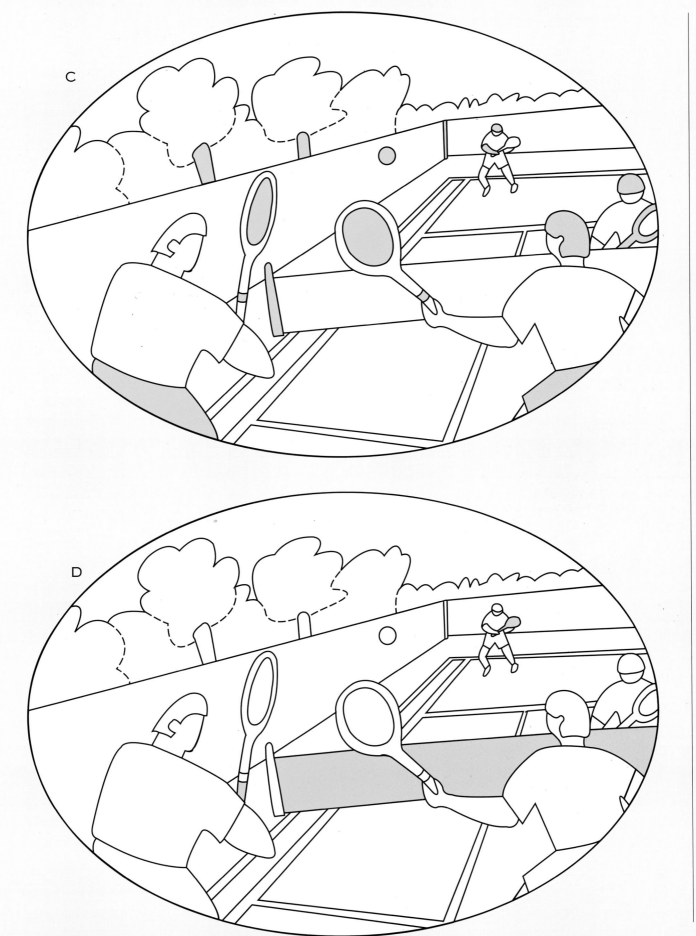

CARD

Card case (pp100-1)
Copy the card, dice and suits stencils, sizing up or down if necessary. Trace separately onto clear acetate as follows: one card; one dice outline and two dice sides (follow the dashed lines); for each suit one large and one small outline, one large and one small inner shape (follow the dashed lines).

DICE

SUITS

SUITS

BORDER

SCROLL

Chess table (pp102–3)

Copy the chessboard (above), sizing to fit, and cut out. Copy scroll and border designs (left), sizing to fit. Trace onto clear acetate.

Sports chest (pp96-7)

Copy the net design (right), sizing it up or down if required. Trace onto clear acetate. Repeats of the pattern can be cut into the acetate or stenciled onto the surface or both. See pages 148-9 for court stencils.

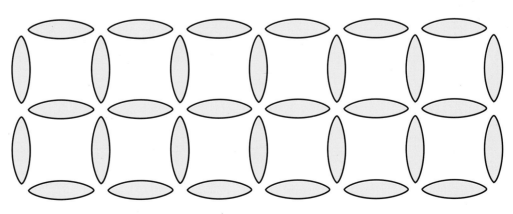

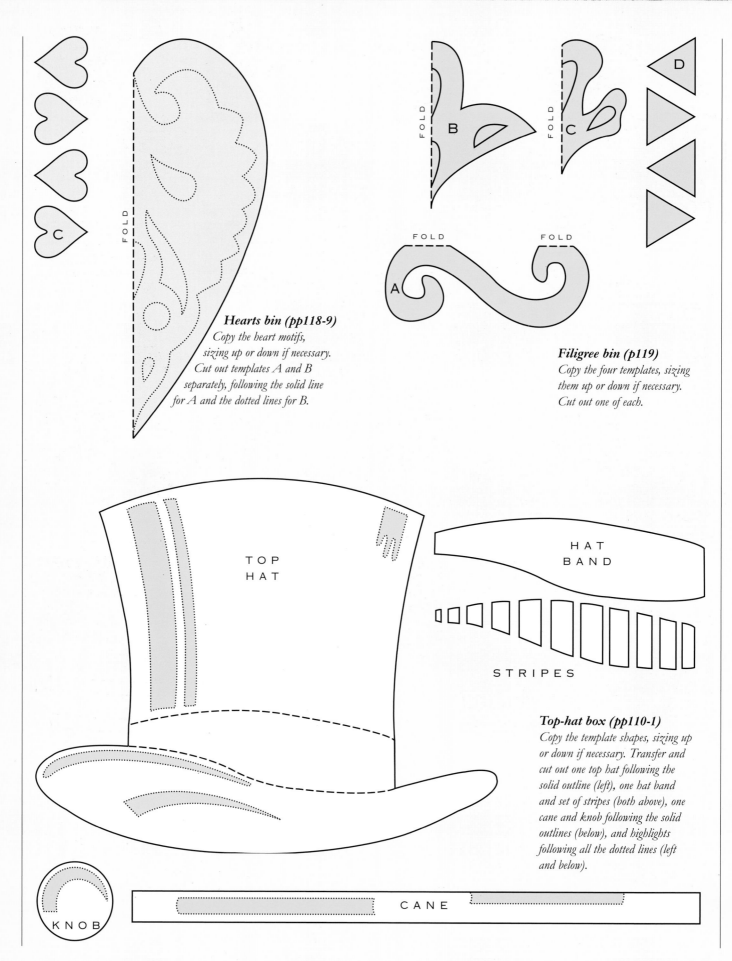

Hearts bin (pp118-9)
Copy the heart motifs,
sizing up or down if necessary.
Cut out templates A and B
separately, following the solid line
for A and the dotted lines for B.

Filigree bin (p119)
Copy the four templates, sizing
them up or down if necessary.
Cut out one of each.

Top-hat box (pp110-1)
Copy the template shapes, sizing up
or down if necessary. Transfer and
cut out one top hat following the
solid outline (left), one hat band
and set of stripes (both above), one
cane and knob following the solid
outlines (below), and highlights
following all the dotted lines (left
and below).

ANIMALS

DANCERS

Dancers box (pp112-3)
Copy the dancers and animals motifs, sizing them separately up or down if necessary. Cut out separately the two animals, the pair of dancers, and the costume details (following the shaded areas).

Steamboat box (p113)
Copy the boat motif, sizing it up or down if necessary. Transfer to template paper and cut out all the shapes separately. The dotted outlines indicate shapes which are stuck down on top of the shape underneath. Follow the solid outlines for the base shapes.

Flower shade (p116)
Copy the flower motif, sizing up or down if necessary. Transfer to colored paper and cut out.

HULL STRIPES

WAVES

FOLD   FOLD

WAVE CREST

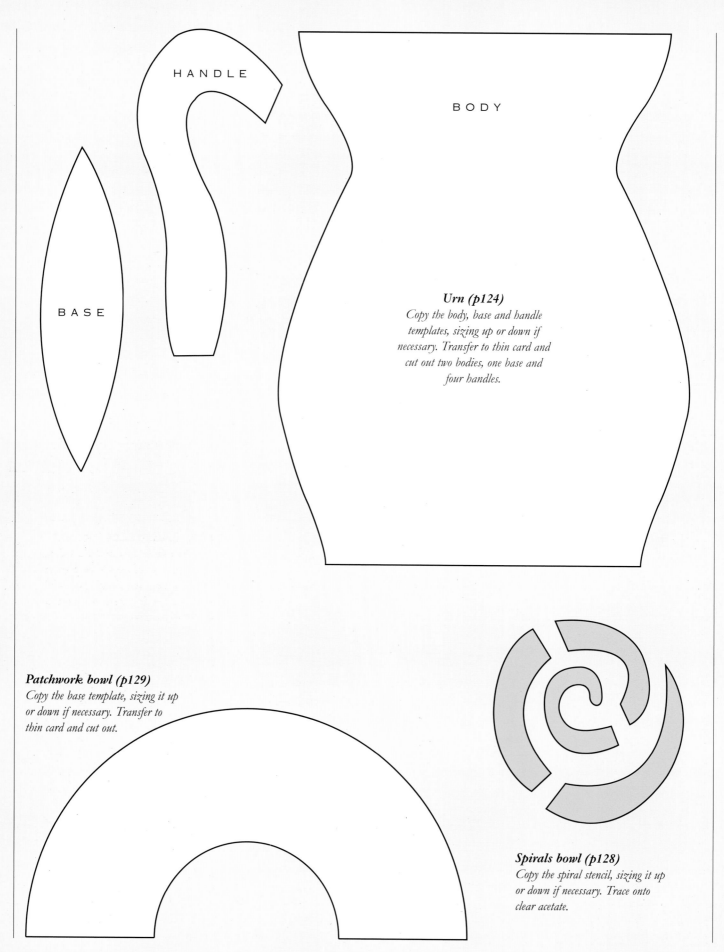

HANDLE

BASE

BODY

Urn (p124)

*Copy the body, base and handle
templates, sizing up or down if
necessary. Transfer to thin card and
cut out two bodies, one base and
four handles.*

Patchwork bowl (p129)

*Copy the base template, sizing it up
or down if necessary. Transfer to
thin card and cut out.*

Spirals bowl (p128)

*Copy the spiral stencil, sizing it up
or down if necessary. Trace onto
clear acetate.*

SIDE TEMPLATE A

BASE TEMPLATE B

Hexagonal vase (p125)
Copy the side and base templates, sizing up or down if necessary. Transfer to card as shown on page 125.

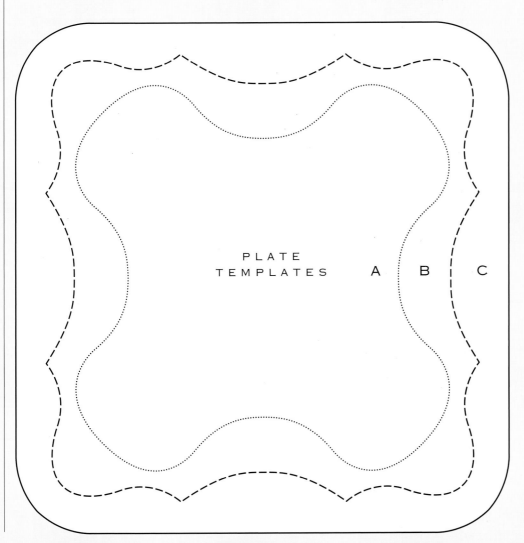

PLATE
TEMPLATES   A   B   C

Square plate (pp130-1)
Copy the plate and rosette, sizing up or down if necessary. Transfer three plate templates to template paper as follows: trace the solid outline for A; the solid outline and the dotted line for B; the solid outline and the dashed line for C. Transfer two rosette templates to colored paper following the solid outline for one and the dashed line for the other.

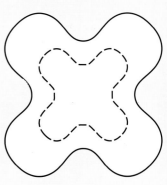

ROSETTE
TEMPLATES

C

A

***Gold scroll frame
(pp132-3)***
*Copy the frame templates,
sizing up or down if
necessary. Transfer
templates A, B and C
(follow the solid line)
to template paper
and cut out one of each.*

B

Green deco frame (p133)

Copy the frame template, sizing up or down if necessary. Cut out the main template following the inner and outer lines. Cut out the small rectangles separately.

INDEX

ACKNOWLEDGEMENTS

Thanks are also due to the following:

I.T. Manager John Clifford
Production Consultant Lorraine Baird
Design Assistants Karen Sawyer, Hallam Bannister
Photographic Assistants Neil Guegan, Sid Sideris
Hand Model Maddalena Bastianelli
Indexer Joel Levy